Matthew

Matthew Goldin

Hesse Press
IV

Contents

  7 Artist Statement
  9 Pilot
 13 Harvard
 29 Barbicide
 35 Clifford's Influence
 43 The Rash
 49 I'm Armed!
 55 Stranglers
 57 Habitat for Humanity
 65 Bad Erotica
 77 30 Rock

Artist Statement

My name is Matthew Goldin. I am a 32 year old, NY-born, experimental mixed media artist and cultural strategist, conceived in the Beverly Hills Hotel—no tattoos, no education. I am passionate about destigmatizing mental health, Wordle, and combating some of the problems we face today.

Growing up, I never joined in on the fun and games that the other kids liked to play. I preferred to depict, with great acumen and to a rapt audience, the gulf between the world of ideas and the quotidian miscellany of chores and little anxieties that constitute this writer's lived experience of a summer afternoon.

Today, weighing in at a whopping 205 lbs, I'm a decent experimental writer-performer and multimedia artist. To put it more simply, I am, for better or for worse, a compelling North American entertainer and prose stylist.

As I've said, my tense, muscular prose is a vehicle for restrained, colorless humor about trips to the mart. Eschewing depth, my style is characterized by surface tension so readers can glide, like water bugs, and laterally discover new ways of laughing and loving.

As a man, I devote a few hours each day to everyday life—and all its quotidian details, so achingly human, that escape the grasping hands of narrative. But as a humor artist, I stay well away from everyday life because it has absolutely nothing to offer me.

Most of the essays in this collection were written between 1991 and 2024, during a period when I was largely kidding. I hope you find them edifying. Please be sure to let me know if you have any feedback. My phone number is (323) 905-7553. I can also be reached online through traditional channels.

Pilot

The premise is very simple. The show takes place in a world that is indistinguishable from ours in every way, except for one small difference. In the world of this show—and keep in mind this is fiction—Bo Burnham cannot move. Aside from that minor detail, the world of the show resembles ours in every way.

Bo Burnham cannot move a muscle. He is alive, but he cannot move his arms or legs. He can breathe and sustain basic automatic life functions, but he cannot "will" any part of his body to do anything. He cannot take action. The pilot of the show establishes this. It shows Bo Burnham perfectly still from many angles. He is brought to different areas and settings, casting new light on his immobility.

It is not clear why he cannot move. This is the great mystery of the show, and the mystery drives the show forward, to an extent. However, the show also focuses on other aspects of this world where Bo Burnham cannot move. For instance, it provides a nuanced take on the international scene. As I've already said, the show takes place in a world almost identical to ours except that minor detail I already talked about. It is extremely realistic in every other way. It covers the lives of everyday people all around the globe. There is sensitivity and humor in its depiction of the way we live now.

Meanwhile, let's not forget, humming away in the background is this somewhat interesting mystery—why can't Bo Burnham move? Undepicted by the show but assumed to be happening in the background, there are, or must be, a few people who are slowly but surely working to get a better understanding of why he can't move a muscle. But the show, if it ever does depict them, makes sure not to do so too narrowly. You see their other interests, their families, the mistakes they make as they navigate their careers and love lives, which are interesting to varying degrees.

There are also more than a few sex scenes, during which Bo, undepicted and likely in another building or city entirely, remains perfectly, perfectly still—but, as I've said, alive and well. The sex scenes, benefitting from this juxtaposition, are extremely erotic, but they also show how awkward things can get when people are at their most vulnerable. The first time you have sex with someone especially can be awkward as all hell. The show shows that.

Eventually—and this can happen once the show has exhausted all potential for depicting the world we live in—there is a twist. Scientists discover why Bo Burnham can't move a muscle. It is not, as one might have assumed, due to any medical problem. It turns out that the reason Bo Burnham hasn't been able to move throughout the show is that he's been tied up with invisible ropes and various other restraints—ball gags, too, it is implied—hence his silence over the years. That's why, while it *seemed* like he couldn't move, actually the whole time he could have been moving around a lot, had it not been for the ropes and restraints.

With bitter irony, the show then reveals that even though, yes, Bo Burnham was capable of movement after all when we thought he wasn't, he now *truly* can't move. Before, he couldn't move due to the ropes. But now, after having been untied, he still can't move. This is because his muscles have atrophied completely due to spending so long tied up by invisible ropes. During the time he was tied up, he wasn't moving around much at all—the show makes that clear as day—so it shouldn't come as a surprise that he didn't get much exercise during that time. As a result, he is now so weak that even sans ropes he is still unable to move a muscle. It is as if the ropes are still there, but they've been internalized on some level.

The pilot establishes the premise and sets us up for everything that comes later. In every episode, Bo Burnham attempts to move or the show leads us to believe that such an attempt is possible. The tension builds. The viewer hopes that it might happen, but they also dread it—because it would mean the end of the show. In the end, reassuringly, no matter what twists occur, the end result is always reassuringly the same.

But, as I've said before, not all of this has to actually be depicted or take place on screen. Much of it is merely implied obliquely. A rhino in the Boston Zoo looking out its window and seeing snow for the first time might, for a sensitive viewer, be enough to convey all of this. Or a scene in which a single dad awkwardly navigates teaching his daughter how to shave her legs—even that might be enough, for an imaginative viewer, to provide a solid sense of Bo's situation. No matter who or what is being depicted, it will be clear, or at least it should be assumed, that Bo Burnham is out there somewhere and, for better or for worse, not moving a muscle. Not even a finger.

It goes without saying, however, that Bo is no more unhappy in the world of this show than he is in real life. In both, he deplores or celebrates his situation to an equal degree. The *only* difference between the world of this show and the real world is that he can't move. He is simply stationary. Is that clear?

Harvard

When I got into Harvard, I was disappointed, not because I'd been hoping for a rejection, but because the unsealing of the acceptance letter was just another task in a series. It didn't feel like the triumphant culmination of years of effort, hope, and maybe more than a bit of luck. I read through the letter, tossed it, and then started messing around with Gmail and my calendar, ensuring I was factoring in all the next steps I'd have to take before September.

When I told my parents, they made me a congratulatory dinner with some extended family. When I told my high school sweetheart, we slowly broke up over the next four months.

The feelings of awe that I should have felt when I was opening the letter came to me belatedly, a few months later, when I first stepped into Harvard's hallowed halls. Rather, a little before that, actually, when my family and I first entered the university's vast parking lot and pulled up to one of its many gorgeous 100% marble curb stops.

Stepping out from the lot a few minutes later onto Harvard's sprawling quadrangle, I sighed with relief. This was certainly no commuter school. The campus was a living, breathing, conscious thing—much like The Zone in Tarkovsky's *Stalker*, an obvious influence. Grand academic buildings, which had undoubtedly been designed by trained architects, towered over the green. I steadied myself with a hand on a marble column, taking in this new world of glimmering, gleaming surfaces, the depths of which I dared not fathom.

My dad put his hand on my shoulder and gave it a squeeze.

"You've earned this," he said. He put his other hand on my other shoulder and began massaging me.

"Not in front of the other students," I said, mortified.

My mom smiled.

"They all have moms and dads, Matthew. I'm sure they are all too familiar with embarrassing parents."

"But you guys are, like, extra embarrassing," said my sister Kath, looking up from the sparrow she was patting, which had alighted near us with a welcoming chirp a few minutes before.

Mom gently but firmly removed her husband's hands from my shoulders. "We're probably just as nervous as you are, Matthew."

"I'm not nervous," I said. "But I do feel just a tad out of place."

Indeed I was. Looking around, it seemed I was the only ginger on campus—aside from my sister, mom, and dad, naturally. I could feel students and deans staring at us. I reminded myself that even if I looked different from the rest of the Harvard student body, we all had one thing in common: grit.

"I bet you'll feel right at home once you're set up in your dorm, honey," said Mom.

"Unless his dorm-mates are fuckboys," quipped Kath, continuing to pat her sparrow, who shivered with evident pleasure. It felt like every knot in its back was coming undone. Truly, this girl had magic fingers.

"Put that down," said Dad, noticing the sparrow. "It belongs to Harvard."

"I'm going to wait in the car," grumbled Kath. The sparrow flew away and joined its brethren in the sky above.

Mom and Dad accompanied me into the dormitory building and up the stairs. The whole place was buzzing with activity. My mom gave my room number to someone who looked older than the other students, and he directed us to my room.

"Yo," said a guy who appeared to be my dorm mate, looking up from his laptop. "The name's Chris."

"Matthew," I replied. "And uh… this is my mom and dad."

"Water?" Chris asked. He tossed me a bottled water. "And maybe for the rents?" He tossed them bottles as well, which they caught radly in midair.

Chris helped my parents and me lug boxes and furniture up the stairs to our dorm. My parents stayed a bit to help me unpack.

"Chris seems like a bright kid," said Mom as I walked them back to the car to say goodbye.

"Yeah," I said. "Though I don't know what's up with the water thing."

"Probably thirsty," said Dad. "Probably just wanted some water." He chugged the rest of his bottled water and immediately littered it on the ground.

I hugged my parents and my sister. We had a whole goodbye scene. At last, they drove off. I picked my dad's empty bottle off the ground and gingerly placed it on top of one of the campus's many burning piles of garbage, designed to convert rubbish to more manageable piles of ash. I was going to miss my family, for sure, but for now, I was relieved to have them gone. I was excited for all that college had to offer.

From the sky, three golden birds viewed me with curiosity.

A frosh, one of them said.

This should be interesting, said the second bird.

The third remained mum, cultivating what it believed to be a "pregnant silence," even though its silence was due to it had nothing to say. This third bird, the most vapid one on campus, had its mind on worms.

Over the next few months, being so good at homework, I excelled academically.

Most of my professors' lectures were about how the peregrine falcon is the fastest animal ever, not the cheetah, which is merely the fastest mammal. The students beside me hardly took notes, just the occasional laconic scribble. *Three school buses*, I saw someone next to me write one day, as our professor delved into the subject of how large blue whales are compared to the size of other large objects.

I thrived socially, bonding with dozens of students, professors, deans, and provosts. All my life, I'd felt like an outsider, but in an environment like this, surrounded by people employed at, attending, or somehow related to Harvard, I seemed to fit right in.

I was chilling one evening with Xavier, a provost with whom I'd become rather intimate. My first week at uni this senior administrative officer and I had bonded over our fondness for shared interests, and we'd been inseparable ever since.

Xavier was telling me about a recent bath, during which he had scrubbed himself so clean that he seemed to look shiny in the mirror afterwards. I passed him the joint. He took a large hit and coughed a little, looking spent afterwards.

"Harvard's dating pool is ass, you know," said Xavier, apropos of nothing.

"I highly doubt that," I replied.

"Trust me," said Xavier. "The dating pool is utter ass. No ifs, ands, or buts about it."

"If that's the case," I asked, "How come so many of us Harvard students end up having kids and settling down?" By this point I was used to this sort of intellectual jousting from the lecture halls and was priming myself for a spirited debate.

"Eh, I dunno," said the provost. "Forget I said anything."

I felt let down. But soon, we moved on to other topics, and I forgot about Xavier's mysterious pronouncement.

But later that night, lying in my bunk below my hydrated dorm mate, the provost's words haunted me. Surely, Xavier had been joking. Probably, he'd been giving voice to some personal resentment. There was no way Harvard's dating pool was ass.

Over the next few weeks, to test Xavier's hypothesis, I developed a crush on a classmate named Meg.

I approached her one day after class. "Meg, there's no one quite like you. I'd like to take you out to dinner or even go "Dutch," if that's what you prefer—say, this Friday?"

"I would love to," said Meg.

We beamed at each other. I felt like kissing her, but a few students and a gaggle of deans were watching with a telescope a few miles away.

"But there's one problem," said Meg. "I don't date gingers. Maybe you want to try the campus' un-picturesque environs? You might find the townies a bit more… open-minded."

"No offense," she added, smiling tightly.

I held back tears as I ran towards my dorm. I fantasised that, however implausible it might seem, the dormant volcano upon which Harvard had long ago been built upon would erupt, and molten lava would spill all over the quad, washing away everything, and with it all evidence of my rejection. Maybe Harvard's dating pool is ass after all, I thought, rooting through Chris' bottled waters. I was parched from crying.

I called Xavier on my iPhone. "You were right about everything," I said. "What should I do?"

Xavier sounded like he had been drinking. "Well, I do have one idea," he said. "But it's a bit unconventional… Have you ever been to Harvard's un-picturesque environs?"

"Sounds scary," I said. "I prefer the finer side of life."

Xavier pondered that. He found it easy to be natural with me — a rare thing for Xavier, who was usually quiet and diffident. And yet, there was part of me that seemed absent. He had the sense that if he brought up something he was truly struggling with, I'd probably speak to him in the same register as always, and this would entrench his loneliness ever further.

"I'm sorry," I said. "I didn't mean to put down your suggestion."

"It's okay," said Xavier.

"I mean… if you think it's a good idea, I'm down to try it."

When we got off the phone, Xavier went outside to smoke a cigarette, ignoring the "No smoking within 20 feet" signs plastered pretty much everywhere around the provost's dormitory. He smiled; it was important to have grit.

The next morning, as I was heading out, Chris asked me where I was going. I told him I was going to the library to hit the books.

"I love hitting those," said Chris, spanking a copy of *A Wrinkle in Time* for emphasis. "Just some wordplay," he joked, waving me goodbye.

Xavier and I had agreed to meet in front of Harvard's southern wall. When I arrived, he sat on a bench, brushing off his Android. "These damned ants," he said, "are driving me nuts... It's the worst part of this uni by far. Dropped my Android on the ground because I'm clumsy AF, and now, of course, it's covered in ants."

"Sorry about the ants," I said sympathetically. "That's always rough."

"Shall we get going?" said Xavier, shouldering his rucksack.

We made our way to the footpath, one of three from which Harvard is accessible by foot. Back in the day, these paths were mainly used by travelling merchants. These merchants didn't just carry their wares. They also brought new ways of thinking, ideas from foreign cities, and even books. Eventually, scholars gathered here, and one thing led to another.

Xavier was explaining this to me in hushed tones, even though no one was around. It didn't look like this footpath was used too much nowadays. It didn't look like this footpath was used too much nowadays.

"It's almost too bad," said Xavier. "About the wall, I mean. Openness, the free flow of people and information, that's what led to Harvard being this way in the first place. Ironic, really, that it would be so closed off now."

"That's the first time I've ever heard that perspective," I said, "and it's an interesting one."

"Thanks," said Xavier, who kept his silence for a while after that.

Right as I was starting to wonder how long we had left to walk (and where we were going specifically), a town came into view. I felt my heart beating really fast.

"Quiet!" said Xavier, even though I hadn't said anything.

A dog emerged from the undergrowth.

"Aw, a dog," I said.

"Don't go near that thing," said Xavier. "You won't love it."

The dog approached us. And to my surprise, Xavier turned out to be right. He was completely unlovable.

When we got into the town square, the first thing we did was remove our clothes. Xavier had brought some outfits that he thought would help us blend in with the locals. I'd never worn pants before. At Harvard, despite being a cishet guy, I'd been required to wear a dress every day — due to woke culture and other aspects of the present day.

One of the locals, who'd kept a respectful silence while watching us strip, approached.

"Harvard boys?" she asked.

"Yeah," I said, "not gonna lie."

"Nice hair," she said, gesturing to my ginger locks.

I blushed, temporarily draining my hair of all red and making me, for a moment, a blonde.

"Thanks," I said.

"Shall we go on?" asked Xavier, completely ignoring the townie.

"Where are you going?" she asked.

"I dunno," I said. "He's in charge."

"Town square," said Xavier curtly.

She offered to show us where it was. Xavier didn't seem super enthusiastic about the prospect, but as it turned out, he didn't have the best idea of how to get there.

The townie introduced herself to us as Alisa or Alice. I immediately forgot which, like an idiot, and was embarrassed to ask her name again. In my head, I called her Alice, because I preferred it.

Alice asked us a few questions about Harvard, but it felt like she was asking out of politeness. She then asked us what we were doing here. Xavier did most of the talking. I appreciated that he didn't mention my feelings of alienation, the growing sense that I was an outcast, or that the Harvard dating scene was ass. I thought that was prudent. We hardly knew this girl, though she was nice enough. The real surprise he revealed was that Xavier had never been outside of Harvard himself.

"Provosts are born on campus," he explained to Alice. "We can only survive two, maybe three days outside of the walls."

"You never told me that," I said.

"You never asked," Xavier countered.

When we got to the town square, Alice introduced us to a few of her friends: Nathan, Samuel, Michelle, Kadie, Richard, Max, Faye, Riley, Maddison, Willy, and Kyle. And William, I believe.

"Sit down," said Alice.

Kyle made an off-color remark about me in another language, and Faye stifled a laugh.

"Cool it," said Alice, turning towards me. "Kyle doesn't mean it, they're just being dumb."

I told them it was okay. It really was. I was feeling extremely shy, but they seemed like good people. I was more concerned about Xavier, who had asked to be excused to go to the bathroom and had been gone for like 20 minutes.

"Number twos take longer than number ones outside the confines of uni," Alice explained to me.

We chatted about this and that for a while. When Xavier returned, someone suggested getting wasted, so we all got into Riley's car and drove around, passing back and forth a bottle of Mang-O-Rita that tasted disgusting. Michelle and Richard had to sit on my lap. Xavier and Willy sat on Kyle's lap. Alice, Nathan, and Samuel sat on Maddison's lap. Riley drove, sitting on William's lap. There was no room in the car for Max, who stayed back to do Sudoku, a form of Japanese ritualistic suicide by disembowelment.

"Haha," said someone in response to a joke. Things were getting crazy.

Eventually, we stopped at a local parking lot—banal concrete, no marble. Everyone stumbled out of the car. All the men had erections from the lap-sitting.

"This is fun," I said. "We don't do this stuff at Harvard. We just go to class, hit the books, party, and have excellent sex in our dorms. I've never driven around drinking Mang-O-Rita while listening to The Polyphonic Spree before. I guess there is a big world out there, huh?"

"Yes, and you're not half bad either," said Alice, elbowing me hard.

"We townies are chill with you," said Samuel, putting his arm around me.

"Hey, you're pretty alright yourselves," I said.

Samuel grinned. "Looks like I've got a friend at Harvard! I'm king of the world!"

Xavier was sitting on a curb stop looking wistful, watching his hands fade. He was disappearing.

"Yo," I said. "We should probably get Xavier back."

But Xavier protested that he was fine. He whispered into my ear that he was having the time of his life. He'd always wanted to do this.

A few of the townies began telling jokes. I'd never seen anything like it. They were making light of everyday situations, poking fun at American civil institutions, and skewering sacred cows. I'd never seen this sort of thing in my uni's lecture halls. This is a whole different kind of discourse, I thought. And it's actually pretty entertaining, if a bit meaningless.

I tried making a joke myself, making sure to punch up, so it ended up being a self-deprecating one. Everyone laughed.

"This is really quite compelling," said Xavier, "But I think I've got to get home."

"We're going to bounce," I said to the crowd.

"Bye guys," said Alice. "Come visit again soon."

I practically had to carry Xavier into the Uber. The provost's feet were transparent, and his vision had started to go as well. The Uber driver seemed skeptical but agreed to take us as long as Xavier promised not to grow fainter and fainter and then vanish entirely.

When we arrived back home, we waved to the snipers on top of the walls, who raised their eyebrows at us and theatrically pointed to their watches. It was 1 in the morning. As soon as we crossed the threshold into campus, I heard a sound like the flapping of wings, and when I turned around, Xavier had returned to his former vividness. He mentioned a mutual interest, and I laughed. My friend was back. We said our goodbyes, and I returned to my dorm and slept through the next day's classes.

I awoke to an email from the ombudsman, who asked me to attend a hearing. Apparently, Xavier was in trouble for leaving campus, and they wanted me to testify against him. "Fat chance," I wrote back rebelliously.

The semester continued, and I began to find my true niche at Harvard. The offices of the Lampoon were located on the edge of campus, under the north-eastern wall. Walking up the steps to the entrance, I observed that even the building looked funny as fuck. A man at the front desk asked what my business was.

"I want to write for the Harvard Lampoon. And I'm not shaving this off," I said, removing my hat.

"Oh, you'll be right at home here," he said, swinging open the door to the sweatshop. Inside, gingers of all kinds—men and women, young and old, sick and diseased—weakly looked up from their laptops, where they were penning humor pieces that revealed not a trace of the writer. As they grinned their welcomes at me, every freckle sparkled like starlight. I threw my hat in a pile of burning rubbish. I wouldn't need it anymore. I'd found my people.

I attended Xavier's hearing, after all, at his request. I was surprised that he'd asked me to speak the truth.

"What is the truth?" I asked him.

"All that education and you don't know? It's the one thing that sets you free," Xavier explained.

When I stood in front of the committee, I told them everything. I confirmed that we'd left campus, that we'd consorted with townies, that we'd joked around a little. Life was good in the un-picturesque environs. There was, I ventured, as much to learn on campus as off campus.

"You certainly have some interesting ideas, Mr. Goldin," said the ombudsman, who was named Sally.

"He's with the Lampoon," an administrator dryly explained to her.

"Ah," said the ombudsman, Sally. "Well, call forth the provost."

Out came a restrained Xavier, led by the burliest administrators I'd ever laid eyes on.

Xavier met my gaze. Thank you, his eyes said.

"Xavier," said Harvard's first-ever female ombudsman, Sally, "you are charged with free thinking on campus, etc. What do you say to these charges?"

If freedom is a crime, said Xavier, using his expressive eyes, then I consider myself the guiltiest man in the world. I believe everyone should have a chance to do what they really want in life.

"So be it," said Sally, the ombudsman.

One of the burly administrators untied Xavier's hands, undid the rope binding his legs, and removed his blindfold and ball gag.

"Be free," said the ombudsman, "if that's what you wish."

A harsh grating sound filled the room as the ceiling parted, letting in a gust of wind.

Xavier stretched his arms—nay, his wings—wide. Soaring suddenly above the other admin, he gave me one last parting smile before disappearing into the sky above.

—

My parents and sister Kath came down to visit a few weeks later, just to check in. "Look," said Kath in the car next to me as we drove off campus to get some lunch with my townie friends, whom I was introducing to my parents. "Look," she said. "Look! A sparrow."

A golden bird circled above us, doing barrel rolls.

"Don't look at it. It's Harvard's sparrow." said Dad.

I just smiled. My parents could believe whatever they wanted to believe. My education was complete.

Barbicide

I noticed a few of the barbers on my block were getting inked. When I first moved here, a few months back, things were different. I'd see them sauntering along the sidewalk, bare arms swinging, heading to their shoppes. I suppose they might have been concealing tats under their clothes—but back then, the thought never crossed my mind. I only had eyes at the time for their scissors, which they carried everywhere. These were beautiful instruments that they used, putting it simply, for cutting hair.

Some of them had tics: in rhythm to their gait, they opened and closed the scissors as if they were walking through a crowd of invisible lads who just needed a little bit taken off from the top. Every time a barber passed me, absentmindedly squeezing their scissors, I would look up at them from my stoop, pretending to still be reading the paper, and admire how the sinewy muscles in their exposed arms tensed and relaxed. But all this changed when the barbers on my block began to get full sleeves. Later, I learned that it wasn't just happening on my block. Things were changing rapidly throughout my entire district.

One morning, I decided to investigate further. As a bald man, I had no excuse for talking to a barber. So, I applied Rogaine to my head for a few years so that I could, at the very least, initiate a conversation. By that point, the change in the barbers was so deep-set and pronounced that one could, with reasonable certainty, assume any illustrated man holding scissors was in the hair trade.

I stepped out of my apartment and sat down on my stoop with the New York Times, surreptitiously observing the activity on the sidewalk through an enormous hole I'd carved into the paper with my own pair of uninspiring consumer scissors. Businessmen of all kinds, long hair flowing in the wind, power-walked along the sidewalk before me, rushing to make their reservations in time.

Gorgeous members of the opposite sex, beautiful beyond belief, sometimes appeared as well. I catcalled them assiduously and indefatigably, commenting on various aspects of their appearance, or sometimes on the nature of desire itself, indirectly hinting at the solipsism of lust and generously implying their interchangeability, so that they wouldn't feel so personally accosted by my language.

A few hours passed in this manner. At 6 am I finally spotted my first barbers: a trio of them ambling down the street and laughing together. They touched their scissors together, clearly relishing each other's company. I wanted to get their attention, approach them, and pick their brains. That was my plan, after all. That was why I was here. Suddenly, I got shy. I looked up at the crown of my head, which was undeniably still bald, and then, straining my eyes still further back, at my power donut. Would this be enough to warrant a conversation? Why was I overthinking this?

By the time I mustered the courage and stood up, the trio had disappeared into a patch of mist. While the barbers themselves could no longer be seen, I could still make out inky black Japanese communiqués as their hosts traversed deeper and deeper through sheets of morning dew.

A few invisible lads joined me on the stoop to play jacks, as children are wont to do. The racket was infuriating and, above all, repetitive. Not fully educated, the children cycled endlessly between the only 2 or 3 thousand words they knew, and by the umpteenth *the* or *I* or *and*, I began to groan and rock back and forth.

I handed the eldest a fiver and told it to go fuck off and buy some candy or something. The child pocketed the fiver and returned to the game. I felt inefficacious and that infuriated me. The very point of a child is to make you feel effectual. To produce one, first of all, is to triumph over impotency. Having them around afterwards, the optional second step, is a boon to one's sense of authority over the helpless. To deny me, that was an affront I couldn't take. So, I confiscated their jacks and threw them onto the street. I figured that even if I couldn't control them, I could, at the very least, scatter their treasures and diminish their capacity for joy. I felt bad doing that, having once been a child. But no longer being one, I also understand the importance of suppressing my essential goodness for the greater cause of social order.

I walked onto the sidewalk away from my apartment building, not daring to look back at the invisible lads. From behind me, I could hear businessmen consoling the sobbing children with various wares and services, supply chains clanking taut behind them.

Unsure what to do with myself now, I followed a long-haired businessman blindly for a while, certain that I'd find myself at the mouth of a barbershop soon enough. I tried to remember the importance of my investigation, but my anger wouldn't abate, and the question of why the barbers had become inked began to seem academic.

The businessman turned into an inconspicuous building, the sort where barbers congregated. The barber pole, its helix of colored stripes rotating with the aid of an electric motor, made it clear as day that I was standing next to a barbershop or at least an excellent facsimile of one.

I walked through a dark alley to the side of the building. The dumpsters overflowed with what looked to be human hair. *So*, I thought, *they basically just throw it out afterwards.*

Standing next to the dumpsters, I extricated a long hair, which I identified as either a hippie's or a member of the opposite sex. The hair seemed to go on and on forever. Ultimately, it was just a glorified string. No wonder the barbers snipped it off. But why the hurry to dump it? I peeked through a small window into the barber's den. There they were, inked up, snipping away. The businessman

I'd followed was there too, reading a magazine and waiting for his appointment.

As the minutes passed, I noticed that everyone in there was aging imperceptibly. It didn't take a genius to figure out that these barbers and clients, so vigorous today, would likely all be six feet under before the end of the 21st century. As mere mortals, they had zero lasting power. None of them were here to stay. At some point, although no one can be sure when and where, they'd get too old for this shit.

Suddenly, it all made sense. Barbers are constantly conscious of death; they snip only dead things. All hair follicles are composed of cells that are no longer living. To placate ourselves and hide from the ugly truth, we civilians who live and work outside the shoppes sometimes talk of "hair growth." Real barbers, of course, see behind such bromides. Yes, there is a living part of the hair, but it is buried, hidden under the skin, every hair an inverted grave.

Making bank in their barbers' dens by snipping ephemera, it's understandable that they'd take solace in the permanence of ink. Once a tattoo exists in this world, it is here to stay.

Yet even a haircut, while temporary, participates in eternity. As the lead barber snipped the long hair of the businessman, it occurred to him that even though this haircut would only last so many days, he had given it to this man and many men like him hundreds of times before. The look would always need to be refreshed. Businessmen would be around forever. There would always be clients. Business was booming.

I walked home. The invisible lads only I could see—these Peter Pans who'd never grow up, and were, in fact, not real—scurried away. Vermin. They'd left the New York Times on my stoop. I picked it up and threw it in the trash. Tomorrow I'd get another paper in the mail, stamped like always with today's date. I'd read it effortlessly, never needing to brush my bangs out of my eyes. I was grateful to be bald. All that was alive in me remained buried within, and I had no graves to snip. I knew I'd never truly understand these barbers, who needed to get inked to participate in eternity. Still, it was trippy and intriguing to observe their goings-on in my rapidly gentrifying neighborhood.

Clifford's Influence

McDonald's is one of the leading quick-service restaurants by sales per unit. With 550 million Big Macs sold globally per year and 60 million downloads of the McDonald's mobile app, it shouldn't come as a surprise that I could be found inside one at various times throughout my life, whether standing remotely in the corner considering the menu or at other times in a bathroom stall on my phone considering the possibility of jacking off as I opened incognito to bypass the nytimes.com paywall.

I was torn between "First Batch of Biden Emails Undercuts G.O.P. Claims" and the promising "Influx of Migrants Exposes Democrats' Division on Immigration." The articles in the New York Times, which are not credited to any individual author but are instead attributed to the collective itself, have sometimes turned me off with their far-left anarchist tendencies. However, as a dilettante with a passing interest in 21st-century civilization, I felt it was important to have all perspectives.

As I was getting to the good part, I heard a rustle. I pulled my pants up and opened the stall door next to mine to see who was inside. It was a small striped kitten lapping at a bowl of milk. He extended to meet my hand as I reached down to pet him. I picked him up and took him outside, tossing him into the bushes so he wouldn't get crushed by the customers in the burger joint.

After performing that mitzvah, I got into my car and just… drove. I enjoyed the feel of the car or vehicle; leather interiors have always been a boon for me. My thoughts resonate better when surrounded by cowhide, much like the notes a soloist plays while sitting in the grand architecture of a concert hall, especially when the audience has been supplied with ample lozenges to suppress their inevitable fits of coughing.

I shuddered as I felt my car drive through a spider web.

I was heading to my partner's home.

After a few knocks, they answered the door. Where have you been? they asked. I couldn't provide a good answer to that. I hadn't been much of anywhere, just browsing really. But now my partner was hectoring me, badgering me with their thoughts and feelings. Of course, it didn't take long for us to have make-up sex. Our relationship would last eight more years.

Spending time with my romantic partner reminded me of my parents—how they also had been relationship types, at least for a time—so I decided to give them a call.

I called my mom first. She updated me about something new that had happened with her dog, a medical issue that dogs sometimes, though rarely, got, but that they universally dreaded. She asked me how I was doing. I evaded the issue and pretended to be cold and distant towards her to get off the phone.

I lay back on the couch and called my dad. With emotion in his voice, he told me he missed me. He had begun to pick up the pieces of his life and even had a partner who encouraged this kind of maudlin affection for his kids. I preferred his affections distant and his language impenetrable.

As he rambled on, I glanced out the window. I spotted a massive dog reminiscent of Clifford. He wasn't red but he was accompanied by a small girl, who stood closely by his side. Their bond was obvious; the dog was a Virgo, and she was a Capricorn. She was patting and massaging his back vigorously.

In the blink of an eye, everything changed. A massive double-decker bus collided with the girl, depriving the dog of a master. The dog lapped at the pooling blood with a concerned look. I jumped off the couch and brought the dog into our home. He would need people who could provide the kind of love he was accustomed to.

Over time, it became apparent that I hadn't just adopted the dog. Along with the dog came his retinue of playmates, work acquaintances, former drinking buddies, advisors, and members of his social support system, a system he'd built up when he was more deeply involved in recovery, which he'd largely maintained since then.

My partner and I enjoyed filling his bowl and handling his kibble. It was an ineffable feeling, running your hands through the little pebbles. We enjoyed taking him for walks around the neighborhood. We enjoyed pulling back the black veil that he now wore, in order to pat him. Still, we were not huge fans of the people he brought home with him.

His advisors were sickly men who wore cheap suits and too much cologne, which they applied from 10ml sample vials. A great mountain of bottles gathered behind our couch, where they had been haphazardly discarded. After Rover's guests left, my partner and I would get out our brooms and sweep the rooms to clear out the fur and Sephora vials. We bickered a lot while sweeping. It became apparent that our relationship wasn't going well, but I think we'd come to a silent understanding. I wasn't sure what it was we understood, exactly, but we understood it well and we understood it silently.

My trips to McDonald's became more frequent. I was waiting in line for the bathroom and reciting the code (9&0QD*) in my head. I *really* had to go. The New York Times article was ready and waiting on my phone but with only 10% battery. I was jittery, looking up at the door, and then down at my phone, 9%, 6%. I needed some privacy to be able to enjoy this article's contents.

After minutes of waiting, I heard a flush and the sound of hands being washed. The door opened. It was one of Rover's advisors, a tall and imposing man with a ramshackle handsomeness. At my house, he only ever had eyes for the dog, and we hadn't talked much, but the impression he gave me was always weak and sickly. This time, however, as he came out of the bathroom, he seemed somehow invigorated. I went in and did my business, but I couldn't help noticing a pile of what seemed to be hair on the floor next to the porcelain bowl. When I was done doing what I had to do, I went in for a closer inspection, something I'd never done before with anything else in my life. It was hair—braids, to be precise. The same color braids that my dog Rover had.

Back at home, my partner tried to initiate make-up sex with me, but because I'd already cum at the McDonalds, I didn't feel up to it. Not knowing exactly how to deal with the situation, I tolerated a hand on my pants as it mischievously crept up toward my crotch. I smiled playfully while thinking of how I could get away without explicitly saying I wasn't in the mood. From behind the couch Rover saved the day, jumping into my lap, blocking my partner's hand. To my chagrin, my partner proceeded to writhe while touching their genital area, or at least gesturing towards it with a vibrator. I focused on patting the dog.

"Are you okay?" My partner eventually asked. I replied that I was okay and that I did have an erection, knowing full well that the presence of the dog would make that hard to confirm. And then, looking pointedly at my partner, I asked, "are you okay?" My partner replied that they weren't, that they had needs, or if not needs, then desires. The dog started panting and asked for a bone. Our needs, one of the random sages wandering our halls paused to explain, are various, and depend very much on the unique situation of the individual.

My partner stormed off, dropping their bone-white vibrator on the ground with a clatter. Rover jumped off my lap and went into a corner with it. I knew my partner would be upset since the vibrator was a custom build, made from ethically sourced cow femur, but the damage was already done. When Rover was satiated with his gnawing, he turned towards me with an unreadable look in his beady eyes.

"Do you want to know more about my master?" he asked, then catching his mistake, "My former master, rather…"

I leaned back and poured myself a lukewarm glass.

My master was a small girl born on the outskirts of the city. Growing up, she was very close to her sister. At school, people often mistook them for each other, which they went along with, often playing delightful pranks. In time, my master's older sister went on to college, leaving my master alone at home with her parents. There, she rapidly became something of the 'designated patient' in her family.

Her parents, whose fighting both daughters had witnessed growing up, and whose sexually transgressive behavior I often witnessed while ostensibly sleeping or grooming myself on their bedside floor, should never have gotten married. The husband often pressured the wife into flogging him, an experience she enjoyed on some level but that ultimately diminished her. Aside from this perversion, the husband was completely conventional, whereas the wife had always been something of a free spirit. I think she felt stifled in the marriage. I doubt her husband noticed anything was amiss in the least.

For him, family life was business as usual. He did everything meticulously right, but his real passion was diligently saving up for little 'gifts' he gave himself for working hard and putting in so many hours at his job. I remember one gift in particular: a BMW he arrived home in one evening. I remember I peed on the front wheel; he made his wife flog me for the transgression—in front of the whole family, no less! Knowing full well the husband's predilection for being flogged himself, I felt a keen sense of shame—as if I, the family dog, had been forcibly made patriarch. This embarrassing moment faded quickly for me, though, as I soon found myself playing in the spray while the husband hosed off my warm piss.

My master, meanwhile, was often absent, being sent to psychiatric wards and other facilities frequented by young girls from middle class backgrounds. Even though her mother was no doubt complicit, her father was the one laying down the law. So, I think over time my master came to side with her mother against her father. By her late teens, she was joining in on their fights, usually 'acting out' in some way that would bring the fights to a close and make her parents a unified front—albeit against her—for one blissful moment.

One day, after an altercation with someone who knew karate, my master's father ended up in a coma, and the grief-stricken mother was afflicted by love for the very first time. Her husband's coma had made him far more palatable. My master, meanwhile, became estranged somewhat from her mother, whose long-suffering condition had been the basis for the intimacy between them.

Her mother responded by becoming closer to her other daughter, who was practicing medicine out in the country. She was practicing, but still hadn't gotten good at it. At one point, during a visit to the countryside, the mother had a little tumble while walking through a patch of mist, and unfortunately, my master's older sister's haphazard surgery wasn't enough to put Humpty Dumpty together again.

Shortly thereafter, my master, essentially an orphan by this point, was out taking me for a walk. That was when the accident happened—after which you entered my life, Matthew. What can I say? You've been good to me. But there's not a day that goes by when I don't think of her.

And yet... And yet there's part of me that's glad, part of me that feels she was put out of her misery? If that doesn't sound cold? Though who knows, who knows... Things could have changed, maybe things would have started looking up for my master...

In any case, it was a life snatched too soon.

After my dog's performative, treat-motivated vulnerability drew to a close, I gave him an absent-minded pat and a fresh bone. I slipped out of the house and made my way to McDonald's, for the second time that day. Rover's story had moved me. I couldn't wait to jerk it to world events under the golden arches.

The Rash

The doctor peered at my rash. "That doesn't look so good," he said.

The eruption, littered with pustules and lichenified patches, was about the size and shape of a very big problem. It throbbed and festered on the side of my torso.

"Does it hurt?" asked the doctor.

"Yes," I said, wincing as his gloved hand prodded my rash with clinical sadism and dislodged a few flakes of dried pus residuum.

"Oh fuck," said the doctor, withdrawing his hand. "Sorry." He sat down and his eyes glazed over.

I put my shirt on. "What's the prognosis?" I asked.

"I honestly have no clue. That's a really, really weird rash."

"Should I be concerned?" I started putting my underwear, socks, pants, vest, and all the rest back on.

"It's probably nothing to worry about," he said. "But I'll prescribe you the sort of thing the Sacklers got in trouble for, just in case the pain starts getting to you."

"Naughty, naughty," I said. "But let's hope you're right about the rash not being a big deal. After all, I'm still hoping to get married one day! If it turns out to be more menacing than you thought, my love interest might spurn me."

"I doubt it," said the doctor. "You're very, very sexy. And I can say that. I'm your doctor."

I turned red.

"Woah," said the doctor. "Woah, woah, woah."

"What is it?" I asked, still red. "Get to the point."

"It's difficult for me to differentiate between your rash and your blush. Your embarrassment and your infection are adjacent. What startled me most of all, though, is that your red rash did not turn a deeper shade of red when you blushed. The only reasonable conclusion would be that your rash is a blush—that you were already blushing and have been for a very long time. And when I told you that you were sexy and you began blushing in earnest, the rest of your body simply caught up."

"Your blush from a moment ago is already beginning to fade," the doctor continued, "but your rash is still red. My guess is that it's the remnant of an old blush that, for some reason or other, never faded. Over time, it inevitably got infected. What you suffer from is known as indelible shame."

"Until I learn to love myself," I said sarcastically to the nerd, "this rash will continue to spread and worsen, huh? And I may even die."

"Bingo," said the doctor. "As a physician, all I can do is treat the pain and try to make you more comfortable. But whether you get better or not is up to you. I could get in trouble for saying this, but your problem is located in the soul. We doctors aren't supposed to meddle with that—we're not even supposed to admit the soul exists—but if what I remember from medical school is correct, it's very very holy, and not to be trifled with."

"Just write me the oxy script," I said, "Or I'll rip you a new one."

"Roger that," said the doctor. "You can go to the waiting room and my secretary will give you your prescription and set you up with a follow-up appointment."

I shook hands with the doctor, who clasped mine firmly and wished me well on my journey of self-discovery. I then got in my car and drove aimlessly for a while. There was nothing to do. What more is there to do in life aside from going to the doctor? Indeed, it was one of life's chief pleasures.

I didn't mind living in this beautiful sci-fi world where medicine was available to all who needed it. In fact, I relished it and tended to make use of tax-funded medical services in my spare time, getting various expensive procedures to ward off rare, impossibly obscure, and quite fashionable illnesses—while of course ignoring my underlying and very real troubles.

Indelible shame, the doctor had said. I let go of the wheel to touch the rash that encircled my body. Pus soaked through both my shirt and my vest. Suddenly, I noticed that my car was careening toward a crowd of vulnerables crossing the street. Grabbing the wheel, I swerved to avoid hitting them. I heard several muffled thank yous from them as my car spun out of control.

Indelible shame, the doctor had said—but I had nothing to be ashamed of. The life flashing before me as my car hurtled off the road was highly presentable and often met with praise. In my mind's eye, I saw my exes, with whom I was still on good terms, I saw my hobby of going to the climbing gym, and I saw my career and side hustles. Oddly, my many, many friends resolutely refused to flash before my eyes Dope, I thought—I wouldn't have to look at other guys while my life flashed before my eyes. I got my phone out and whipped up a quick Facebook status.

Just as I was clicking "send" on the post, my car crash concluded. My car had hit and destroyed something of inestimable value, but at least I was safe. I jerked the seatbelt out of my porous red abrasion, wincing as I freed myself from that which had saved my life. There was a tap on my passenger seat window.

"You okay?" said a kind police officer.

"Why? Do I not seem okay?" I asked. I always trolled the men in blue.

"I saw you wincing after the crash."

"Must have been someone else," I joked.

He acknowledged my humor and then helped me out of the car.

"Oy, you're bleeding something awful," said the pig.

"No, it's just a rash. I suffer from a condition known as 'indelible shame.'"

"Oh, really? Me too!" He unbuttoned his bulletproof vest and out bounced a festering pot belly. His raw red flesh had the texture of honeycomb. I was amazed that hair could still grow there.

We bonded for a few minutes about having the same rash. The pig and I shared a beer by the side of the road.

"I believe I might be part of the LGBTQIA community," confessed the pig. He hadn't told anyone this before, only his journals.

It was times like these that I despaired of having only transactional relationships with other people. Most of the time, the results of that approach were awesome and productive—but after his disclosure, I felt obligated to share something from my inner life—and I was drawing a blank, so I lied.

"I used to sneak into kindergarten classrooms during naptime and papercut the kids," I fibbed, while the officer looked at me sympathetically.

"I may be a violent one-dimensional man," he said, "but I understand that I am this way because of intergenerational trauma. I've done a lot of work to understand myself better. When I commit state-sanctioned acts of senseless brutality, I do so while in possession of a rich inner life."

"Interesting stuff. Shall we exchange contact info on WhatsApp?"

"Do you actually want to be friends with me?" asked the cop. "Or are you trying to do so only because the relationship might enrich your inner life?"

"I'm honestly not sure," I answered, looking down at my shoes.

"I'll let you off with a warning," he said. "Do some self-examination. If you don't, you might end up paying the cost next time."

The officer drove off and eventually disappeared over the horizon. I took an Uber home. By the time I got there, my Facebook status had accumulated almost a million likes.

I'm Armed!

There I stood, 6'3, body covered in permanent tats, with a very real gun in hand—which I was ready to use against an innocent. The shopkeeper at whose head the gun was aimed couldn't help but notice my air of quiet menace.

The honest laborer looked up at me, and it occurred to him that even if I was doing a very bad thing to him, it didn't necessarily mean that I was a bad guy. In some remote corner of his mind, it occurred to him that there could, on some level, be something good about me. I could have a few chill aspects.

There was something pathetic, though, he decided, about this train of thought. It bothered him that he wanted to be internally noble at this time. What use was there sympathizing with a guy like me, who was robbing him and might end up killing him? Sure, he could imagine my material needs, the probability that I had loved ones—but why was he doing that kind of imaginative labor at a time like this? Insofar as he was concerned, if he valued his life, I was a piece of shit. It would be far more based, even if less spiritually accurate, to despise me.

"Empty your cash register!" I intoned, my muscles rippling as the syllables rocked my body.

"Whatever you say, kike," said the small business owner, experimenting with hostility. He was surprised at himself. There was something to this, he thought—being a bad guy. He wasn't certain if I was Jewish or not. My mom, with whom I stood, appeared to be a shiksa—so maybe I was only half Jewish, and technically not Jewish at all since the religion is matrilineal. Honestly, though, the only reason he'd gone down the antisemitic route, when it came to it, was that he just didn't feel quite comfortable with other slurs, except maybe homophobic ones, but he always felt kind of compromised saying those, ever since he'd heard that homophobes are themselves gay.

I squeezed my mom's hand with my non-gun-wielding hand. We're going to get you the medicine you need, Mom, my squeeze communicated. The bond between mother and son was, for anyone who treated their mom right, pretty epic—to the point where language was no longer needed, as long as mother and son remained in unbroken physical contact. This was something I'd always felt strongly about, as a good son, and as a pervert. My mom's hand, cold and frail, responded with its own message: I trust you, son, and I love you unconditionally—I just know you'll get me the medicine I need...

The shopkeeper opened the cash register. Coins, trinkets, and treasures galore sparkled under the fluorescents. A gentle sea breeze jostled them slightly, almost deafening us with the resulting jingles and chimes. My imagination went wild, and I pictured in my mind's eye the various procedures and cures these gems and jewels would procure for my ailing mother. She looked up at me, her muscular, tatted son, armed to the teeth, and she had nothing but love in her eyes. For her, my essential goodness was not, and never would be, up for debate. Therefore, I just had to keep her alive.

"Put all that in the bag." I said, prodding the shopkeeper with the *hole* area at the end of the tube of my gun.

The shopkeeper raised an eyebrow. My New Yorker tote bag was the big elephant in the room here, it seemed to him. Even under duress, he felt a little compromised holding it. Initially, when I'd first come in and informed him of the robbery, he'd been peeved and scared—but when it became clear after a minute or so that I planned to have him empty all his valuables into a big New Yorker tote bag, he'd felt embarrassed. He wasn't sure if visibly cringing was going to imperil his life, so he'd made a big show of being a subscriber, being a reader of the New Yorker, which was partially true.

He felt dirty after giving me that spiel, realizing he was sucking up to me, a horrible thug. It reminded him of every other time in his life when he'd smiled while passing someone who had just the other day been rude, cruel, or disrespectful to him. This kind of accommodating behavior, he'd come to realize, just perpetuated these patterns. It made people think it was okay to walk all over him. In this case, it might even make me, an armed robber, believe it was okay to kill him. To survive, the shopkeeper mused, it might make sense to make a little show of strength, of having a backbone.

"Really?" he said with trembling contempt. "This bag? Are you sure?"

The shopkeeper thought about saying something antisemitic again, but all of that felt very remote and absurd considering the very real materiality of the New Yorker tote bag.

"Yeah, fill up the bag,' I grunted. I'd never been much of a talker. But the language I did use was economical, straight to the point. There was a weight behind my every utterance. You couldn't help but listen. And hell, even if you didn't like me, you had to at least respect me.

The shopkeeper began to fill the bag. He tossed gems and coins in carelessly. Having something to do with his hands was a bit of a relief. He kept his eyes on my mom and me. It was obvious to any observer that she was my mom, because she kept silently squeezing my hand and wordlessly communicating short messages to me such as: I love you, my only son, and it means the world to me that you would go through all this just to help your ailing mother.

This time I didn't squeeze her hand back. I'd had enough of these games. As the shopkeeper filled the bag, I took this opportunity to kiss my mother on the mouth.

"But I'm sick," she said, pulling away after a few minutes. "You'll catch it."

I wiped some of the germs off my mouth with my shirt sleeve. Some of them bounced onto the floor and scurried away. They were green.

"We're all sick on some level," I grunted, my language as economical as ever—its primitive idiom and halting cadence belying a deep well of thought. "But only because we live in a sick society. To be sick is to be unfit, to find it hard to function. In a sick society, individual health means adapting oneself to social sickness. For a person who functions well in America—under capitalism—this is a dismal kind of wellness, no? So yes, mom, you are sick, I am sick... But I wouldn't have it any other way."

The shopkeeper found this discourse infuriating.

"Is that supposed to be a justification for infringing upon my rights?" he asked. "Even if you're right on some level, I resent the implication that I'm somehow spiritually stunted just because I'm a decently high-functioning family man and merchant. Your criminality doesn't put you in some privileged position. Committing a burglary isn't inherently a critique of capitalism or of the ordered world we live in. As someone who lives in this ordered world, who is intimate with it, I'm very aware of its flaws—and, though I have crises of confidence like anyone else, I honestly do believe it is from this position that I'm best able to make a difference, however small."

I didn't respond. All of this went completely over my head. I just kept staring impassively as the shopkeeper talked animatedly about this and that, filling my New Yorker tote bag with his hard-earned dough. The guy had an exceedingly punchable face. I could tell he felt superior to me. But I suppressed my violent urges. The important thing right now was to get out of here as quickly as possible before the cops came.

Handing me the bag at last, the shopkeeper realized that it was all over—that he was safe, and that the only thing he'd lost was money. His heart had been beating quickly for fifteen minutes, but that would subside, and this whole thing would soon crystalize into an anecdote, one that would be worth every penny lost. There was something pathetic about that, he thought, the notion that he would be telling this story later at parties, glossing over, of course, his brief foray into antisemitism. Looking into my mother's cloudy eyes, obviously blind, the shopkeeper felt, for the first time in his life, truly seen.

The policeman hearing all this, hours later, thought to himself that life truly was a gift. Human connection is a mysterious, bittersweet thing. The city of Los Angeles is a lonely city, each car a fortress of solitude moving in tandem with countless others. To be alone has its comforts, but we all have a desire to crash, to have our solitude punctured, to let in less stale air, however harsh.

To experience another human being in all their fullness, to experience real connection, is to know violence, in all its horror and poetry. Yes, violence. For what is a gun if not a way to connect with another from afar? Something in the shopkeeper's story had touched the police officer. It was just too bad that he, the officer on the scene, would have to arrest everyone involved—and maybe even fill us all up with lead.

Stranglers

I use my home every night against horrible men. These awful men, prowling the streets, could easily get me—but when I use my home's walls on them, they find themselves completely blocked.

Strangling nothing, least of all me, these violent types wander the perimeter of my home, bereft of purpose. I recognize that class plays a role in this. Not everyone is allowed in, but because I have the keys, and because I'm in, it is clear to me that I am no strangler.

Homes keep the world out, but a larger one keeps less of the world out, because it uses up more world, leaving less to exclude. In an ideal world, I would live in a home no larger than I am. That way, everything that isn't me would be outside it. But I would be in it. In an ideal world, all the world would be outside of me, and I'd be totally at home in myself. I'd look outside at the world around me, observing the stranglers and creeps, using eyes, windows, binoculars, and a fearful imagination.

I don't understand stranglers, all I know is that they give me the ick—and that they're not in my home. I feel nothing, at all times, around my neck. Sometimes I feel no hands clasped around my throat for hours and hours. After a certain amount of time, you get acclimated to the absence of them. You get used to it. You stop noticing you're not being strangled. A whole lifetime can go by. But then, looking back, maybe there were moments here and there...

Not all stranglers have horrible huge hands. Some are chill, at least as far as their hands are concerned. Their hands look fine or at least acceptable. At the very least, they don't look *off.* However, they are still unethical, due to malice located in the strangler's mind. The mind of a strangler is inclined toward harmful negative actions concerning necks. Stranglers commit horrible acts—but only as far as necks are concerned. They only go for that one spot. That's because they're obsessed with strangling victims to death. It borders on an obsession for them. If they're doing it as a joke, it's a joke stranglers have taken too far.

If you want the literal truth, almost everything in this world is unstranglable. All objects except necks rebuff stranglers. Stranglers feel impotent for this reason. They are not at home in this world. They can't strangle anything here, pretty much. That's why they seek human company.

Habitat for Humanity

Most of my life took place outside the zoo. Almost every waking moment of my life was a moment spent elsewhere, doing activities distinct from and unmistakably other than strolling through the zoo with my friend Amy while admiring the gila monsters, hippos, African penguins, lemurs, and monkeys. However, on this particular Saturday afternoon that was exactly what I was doing.

Amy objected to the cages. "Metal is so pedestrian," she said.

"Agreed," I replied. "But if the animals were kept in cages made of diaphanous silk, we'd probably be just as unsatisfied with that."

"I suppose we're never satisfied with the status quo," Amy mused. "And the funny thing is, everything new and different eventually becomes the status quo, doesn't it?"

"Exactly," I said. "Even my biggest accomplishments have left me feeling a bit empty afterward. There's a surge of dopamine followed by a steep drop below baseline. You catch up with yourself. The good you sought, which was once a surplus, becomes just another aspect of your life, just another thing to worry about or lose. And there's no turning back. People say you should be grateful for what you have but imagining you're hungry and homeless to appreciate having food and shelter never really does the trick. Ultimately there's nothing worth pursuing. We all have our fantasies, sure, and pursuing those fantasies is fun—but it's more about the thrill of the chase. Actualizing any of them just neutralizes the joy. But, that's probably just my clinical depression talking."

"No, no," said Amy. "That's actually very well-articulated."

One of the monkeys grinned at us. I felt a healthy sense of contempt for the animal—because I was older than it. I grinned back.

"I've got to say," said Amy. "You don't look too clinically depressed right now."

"Well, I'm at the zoo!"

"Good point," said Amy, walking on to the next cage.

I was watching Amy more than the other animals. I'd invited her to the zoo a week prior after she'd told me that she'd never had the opportunity to see life at its most restrained. I loved seeing creatures behind bars, and obviously, I was hoping Amy would love it too. I hurried to catch up with her. Amy had moved past the monkeys and was now admiring a tigress from a distance.

"It's so fierce," she said.

The tigress was uncharacteristically uncaged, and it was acting savage AF toward a few nearby families.

"It is fierce," I agreed. "But I hate watching this sort of thing."

"Okay phew," said Amy. "That's a tremendous relief. I didn't want to say anything because I know you're a huge fan of this place. But yeah, a lot of the tigress' actions are a bit cringe, especially its behavior toward those poor families over there."

"No, no, I feel the same way," I assured her. "It's never like this. This is an anomaly if there ever was one."

Amy and I approached a zookeeper and asked how the tigress had escaped.

"It's a mystery wrapped in a riddle inside an enigma," he quipped.

We laughed and explained that we were LA-based creatives who "got" that kind of humor.

We watched for a while as the zookeeper did his job vis-a-vis the tigress.

Afterward, Amy and I walked to a concession stand to buy some lemonades and get away from the gore, which we found even less palatable with the sun beating down on us. It was, I've neglected to mention, an unusually hot summer day.

We were both dehydrated, and Amy jokingly said she was dying of thirst. I rolled my eyes. This was typical of Amy, leaning into the joke. She began to chug her Gatorade and spilled it on herself as she laughed.

"You're an animal," I said. "You should be in one of these cages!"

"Rawr," she said, gesturing to the outdoor cafeteria where we were sitting. "So far this is my favorite part of the zoo."

"So basically, you're saying you wish we'd gone to a restaurant instead?"

"Kinda?"

"Oh come on," I said. "There's way more to see, try to have an open mind. There are some really cool animals behind bars here—even some exotic creatures from Mexico and Africa!"

"Now that I gotta see," said Amy, who owned a globe in her apartment.

We spent a few hours looking at the gators. I took a photograph of Amy in front of the gator habitat with the flash on, and accidentally startled a gator, who let out an ear-piercing scream. Startled by the gator's yell, Amy dropped what remained of her drink, spilling it all over an ant.

"Domino effect," I said, offering Amy my lemonade, which I didn't really want anyway because my dad is pre-diabetic and I occasionally worry about that sort of thing.

"So what is it you love about the zoo, Matt?" asked Amy as we were walking away from the gators, who by this point we completely understood.

Amy was the only person I allowed to call me Matt; she did it sometimes to tease me. I enjoyed being made fun of; tolerating ridicule helped me convince myself I wasn't pompous.

"Can you repeat the question?" I asked.

"Crap, I actually forgot what I was asking," said Amy. I couldn't tell if she was being passive-aggressive or had genuinely forgotten.

"Maybe you should get your brain checked out for dementia," I kidded, making sure that my tone was only 5% hostile, so I'd have plausible deniability.

"That's not funny," said Amy, who at 91 years old prided herself on engaging with culture, keeping up with the times, and always learning new things.

"I'm sorry," I said. "Let's go visit some more beings."

"Works for me," said Amy. "You know I can't stay mad at you for long."

"That's probably due to the dementia," I said, unable to help myself.

"Idiot," said Amy, smiling despite herself. "But yeah, I'm down to see one more creature before we go. Maybe the vultures?"

We considered the possibility of walking out of the zoo off toward the horizon and finding ourselves eventually in a desert, with no food, water, working phones, or sense of direction. Eventually, we predicted, despair would set in. As our bodies became weak and desiccated, we'd stop talking, moving forward with a growing sense of futility, punctuated by moments of violent hope and magical thinking. After that—and there's no guarantee of this of course—we might spot buzzards. And we'd at last have the chance to observe the fascinating creatures doing their thang.

"Problem is," she continued, "I'm sort of under a time constraint. Otherwise, I'd love to. I'm supposed to go over to Misty's place later to practice Spanish."

"It's awesome you're learning Spanish," I said.

She thanked me and said that her Spanish had already proven useful at the zoo, as she'd been able to complete several Duolingo lessons while waiting in line earlier for the bathroom. If she didn't know a little Spanish, she wouldn't have been able to do that.

We decided to go to the zoo's fly exhibit, mainly because it was so close by, inasmuch as it was everywhere. Tons of people were pressed up against the glass, watching gnats and horseflies as they buzzed around and occasionally landed on meats and dung that had been placed artfully around the terrarium. Amy pointed out a placard that went into detail about the feng shui principles that had informed the design of the flies' habitat. The landscape architecture had been a huge undertaking, a years-long affair beset by significant controversy.

She sat down on a bench to Google it, obviously more interested in the background of the exhibit than in the flies themselves. It turned out the exhibit had been sponsored by some LGBTQIA organization—and apparently, a lot of zookeepers are as straight as an arrow, so there had been some pushback. And when the exhibit architects had decided to follow the principles of feng shui—right at the start of Covid, mind you—there'd been additional backlash because of anti-Chinese sentiment.

"Only in America…" said Amy, rolling her eyes.

Looking at the flies buzzing around was ally behavior. We watched them feed and lay eggs on feces, garbage, decaying animals, and other filthy places.

"What is it you love about the zoo?" asked Amy. "I just remembered the question."

"I've seen a lot of people critique the zoo for being cruel or unnatural—people who say that we can never really simulate the natural habitats of the creatures we cage up here, and they're right, of course. But, what of our natural habitats? Where do humans belong? I watch a helluva lot of comedy films that satirize office life and bourgeois domesticity, so you shouldn't be surprised to hear me say that those spaces are not conducive to freedom. I'd argue that the zoo is the preeminent site of human agency because it is where we go to parody nature and play god. Only when we're at the zoo, where the natural world is oppressed and obscenely displayed before us, can we be said to be in our natural habitat."

"It's like that old joke about how zoos are actually caging us humans, and it's the animals observing us," said Amy.

"I've never heard anyone say that," I said. "But yeah, that's why I like the zoo and that's why I take my pseudo-dates here."

"Gotcha," said Amy. "Well, it's been pretty fun! Thanks so much for inviting me!"

That evening, throwing back drinks with Amy, her Spaniard friend Misty, and a few other friends at a local pub, I reflected on how I hadn't truly answered Amy's question at all, because I hadn't meant a single word I'd said. But at least I'd shown her a good time. I honestly didn't really like the zoo either, but I always forgot about that and ended up going every few years. I swatted a fly and felt a little surge of dopamine.

Bad Erotica

Male

Watching my sex partner from across the hall, I couldn't help but imagine her naked. In my mind's eye, she was exactly what I'd always imagined.

After about 5 hours, we decided to chill at my place for a bit.

Once we were there, I knew shit was about to get real. After all, it was all but impossible to be in my home without at least passing by my sack once or twice.

There we sat, awkwardly exchanging glances on the threshold of said sack. All I had to do was get her in it. I felt my heart beating fast in my chest. I was about to have sex…

"Shall we strip?" she asked mischievously.

"I'm down," I said. I imagined a nerd saying "no" and how badly *that* would have gone.

I meticulously removed all of my clothes, careful to avoid any emotions. She looked at me coldly. A blonde. Just how I liked it.

Aaaaand it was official: the chick was completely naked!

"I'm ready for you to take me now," she said, spreading her pussy for me.

"This is gonna be easy,' I opined, readying my cock. I put it in my hand and jacked it. I had to get hard for her no matter what. I wanted to be really hard so that there'd be no doubt whatsoever in her mind about what had gone down after all was said and done.

I continued jacking it for a while until I was as hard as a rock. That was when things started getting interesting.

"Let's do this thang," I said, thrusting with relative ease into her hole.

I thrust in and out for a decent chunk of time. Then I suggested we try a different position!

She got on all fours. Her unspecial asshole looked exactly like mine, or my dog's, or any other. That sort of shit turned me off.

"Sorry," I said.

"All good," she said, beginning to turn me on again.

Unfortunately, I couldn't enter her right away. She needed to be lubed up.

"Got lube?" she asked, parodying Got Milk in a way that made her seem like girlfriend material for a second.

"Yeah… I think I got some," I said, searching through my shit until I found a bottle of some of that shit.

"Here," I said, handing it to her. "Ready?"

"Yup!" She finished applying it.

I got back inside.

It was around then that I made her cum. Hard.

"Keep going!" she said enthusiastically, while I quietly busted inside of her.

Afterward, we relaxed on my old sack and felt horror...

"You on the pill?" I asked, "It's just a question."

"No," she said. "No pill, no nothing."

"This isn't gonna go very well, is it?" I asked, feeling increasingly concerned.

Shortly thereafter, consciousness began to stir in her womb.

Fetus

"Bored, bored, bored, bored, bored!" I exclaimed, silently.

I pressed experimentally against the inner epithelial layer of the uterine wall. Nope. Nada. I was stuck here with nothing to do.

With vague alarm, I recognized that I was yet another entity being added to the world's mix. My stage of development was already trying my nerves. So solipsistic. Just me, me, and more me. I had the sense that even after birth, it would be much the same—that delusions of reference would always plague me. My environment would expand, sure, but it would always remain commensurate with me.

My personality was amorphous. To take shape would be a form of dying, a genocide of possibilities. Tragedies would whittle me down and give form to my life story, but what I feared most was the ambient suffering, the quotidia of little disappointments and discomforts that shielded themselves in vagueness, escaping the grasping hands of narrative, denying one the salve of memory's meaning-making machine. These banal pains would, of course, constitute a greater quantity of pain over time than any life-defining tragedy. If suffering could be quantified, which of course it couldn't, then the sum of every uncomfortably chilly night throughout my future life would dwarf the anguish of one day feeling my parent's hand grow cold in my own.

My biological sex already pissed me off: male, of course, like my father.

I kicked the uterine wall again. I felt my mother, my everything, wince around me. How many times throughout my life would *this* pattern repeat?

"Abort me!" I screamed, or tried to.

But my consciousness was already becoming quite sophisticated indeed, and I knew that at this point it would be morally repugnant, if not yet a crime, to liquify me. I prayed for a miscarriage instead. I found that prayer was possible even without a concept of God. It manifested as a kind of attention, a graceful self-forgetting, uncomplicated by divine glory.

When I contemplated the idea of a miscarriage, I felt a sneaky thrill, like the kind I would get many years later walking into a party, scoping things out, and then leaving before anyone noticed me. To escape the world without ever having seen the sun's dirty fingerprint smear its way across the sky even once—that would be an accomplishment.

But just as I couldn't will Mom into having an abortion, I couldn't ensure a miscarriage either. Even a hunger strike was out of the question logistically. After all, I was being fed involuntarily by an umbilical cord. Could I use it to hang myself?

Just as I was losing hope, I felt an oafish hand pressing on the other side of the wall. It was Dad's. He hadn't flown the coop?

Dad's presence gave me hope. Maybe he would lose his cool and *get physical* with Mom. He seemed like the type. That would be a sure-fire way of inducing miscarriage and terminating my existence.

My birth, that inevitability prophesied by Mom's stalwart OBGYN—could be prevented. To thwart fate, I would have to enrage Dad.

Sperm

As for the rest of us, we dripped out of her pussy, down her thigh, into her crack, and onto the sack. Others of us continued dribbling ever so slightly out of his cock. As we dried, we thought back to our final flight, from one darkness to another. We were messengers. And we had all failed. Not only that, but we'd never know if any of our brethren succeeded.

"You're a morose lot," I said, looking at my fellow comrades. I was drying like the rest of them, but I was determined to do it my way. The problem with us sperm, I thought, is that we identify too much with the mission. But for me, there had always been more. There was art, poetry, philosophy—even religion.

As I dribbled into the crevice of some cellulite, I waited for the final reckoning. The man from whence I came was soon to return with a rag, which he would wipe over me, absorbing me, before tossing it into the laundry bin, where I would complete my desiccation process over an untold number of days or even weeks, eventually becoming a brittle kind of "crust."

I thought about Jesus Christ: he too had lived a short life. Surely in his final spread-eagled moments, he'd thought about entities like me: feeble, meek sperm. The son of God had been one of me once—just an idea. Maybe he still was one. I did not doubt that there was a place for me in Heaven above.

But had I, or the possibility I represented, been good?

I knew I ought to check my overweening certainty that I was indeed good. And yet it seemed this certainty was the one thing that was mine—my birthright. My simple and uncomplicated life, devoid of worldly pleasure, which both began and ended alongside my monkish brothers, was entirely devoted to a single mission. I carried out my duty, yet my mind was somewhere else, attending to matters eternal.

God, I knew, or I'd heard, was a man. He was someone who watched me dry with compassion, who understood who I was in all my uniqueness, and yet somehow managed to do this for every one of us. Let His false priests and sycophants declare fornication a sin. I was fornication's unwitting accomplice, its helpless issue, and was not to blame.

If God had a cock to suck, its discharge would be innocent: each sperm would represent a possibility, neither wrong nor right, of His existence (or Her's).

My soul trembled (or, I trembled, for soul was all I was). I, a mere set of genetic instructions, pure idea, trembled, never to live and never to die but guaranteed a place in Platonic heaven. Jesus Christ had also been a sperm once, and He died for my sins no less than for anyone else's.

During post-coital clean-up, they missed me with the rag. No matter. Within minutes, I'd formed a sort of sticky residue on her inner thigh. In fact, I functioned as a sort of moisturizer for her skin.

My possibilities foreclosed, I experienced nonbeing as fact.

I awoke in the Kingdom of Heaven. God beamed at me, shining brighter than any metaphor.

"You," he said. "You are home."

"No shit, Sherlock," I said, testing my angel wings and blasting the whole area with wind.

Fetus

Dad put his hands on Mom's belly. She was wearing a tank top that he found sexually attractive.

"I can feel him kicking," he lied.

I hadn't kicked for days. I'd hoped that this would make her panic, constrict her breathing and stymie my development.

"Is he really kicking?" said Mom, beaming. Non-consensual warmth surged into me through the umbilical cord. Serotonin and dopamine that I couldn't spit out.

Presumptuous prick, I thought to myself, he had given my mother hope. His hand drifted up to her tits.

"They're getting bigger," he said with a sly grin. "Even bigger than they already were."

"Oh, you," she said. "You're incorrigible."

"I am, am I?" he said, pinching one of her nipples above the tank.

Ouch! I felt her pain but without any of the erotic aspects she was experiencing. I wasn't into guys…

"I kind of want to suck them," said Dad, lifting Mom's tank and putting her breast into his mouth. They'd gotten only nominally bigger. He just liked the idea that they would be getting bigger throughout the pregnancy. That idea was sufficient to turn him on. It was true what they said: the most powerful erotic organ in the body is the brain. This is why erotica, as a genre of literature, has always been more about ideas than anything else.

Mom whimpered while Dad sucked. She shut her eyes. Was she thinking of me?

Though I intended to avoid birth and never even try suckling her breasts, I couldn't help but feel annoyed at the way Dad aped my ostensible future behavior. Those tits were meant to nurse me. This predator who'd knocked her up could admire them from afar, if that was his thing.

Dad slipped his other hand into Mom's yoga pants. She wasn't wearing any underwear either. Dad assumed the absence of undergarments was intended as a provocation. I knew her better. Mom was just depressed. He tried to slip a finger in. Close, but no cigar. He rubbed for a minute, trying to activate the area.

"I want you," Mom sighed. Dad looked up and grinned, pausing in his labors.

"I guess I can't get you pregnant again, can I?"

Mom exercised her agency with a sexy-coded look; Dad dropped drawers. He was harder than steel! He spat on his cock, pushed my mom down on the bed, pulled her yoga pants all the way down to her ankles, and stuck it in.

I saw the head of his penis as it thrust in and out of my territory within Mom's abdomen. Dad's penis was small. Yet another reason I didn't ever want to be born. Nonetheless, it was long enough to continually poke me in the arse.

"Faggot…" I muttered. "You into this shit?"

Dad's pathetic pale cock pressed against my undeveloped asshole. That gave me a brilliant idea. I turned around in the womb to face the penis head-on.

"I just felt something!" shouted Mom.

"I bet you did," said Dad.

His thrusts were getting faster and faster.

Facing the penis, I got ready to pounce. I had to time this right. I wouldn't have an opportunity like this again anytime soon, especially since my dad had already mostly lost interest in my mom sexually.

His malefactor slid in again. "Ugh," groaned Dad, soaking in the moment and in Mom.

Now! I leaped forward, slicing the head of Dad's penis with a single long coke nail.

The taste of metal made me gag as blood muddled the amniotic fluid.

"What the fuck!" Dad screamed, withdrawing.

"Keep going!" said Mom. She touched herself, assuming Dad was putting on a cock ring or tending to some personal matter. But she was too wet. She brought her hand up and was startled to see blood.

Dad stood dumbfounded, getting weaker by the moment. "What have you done to me?" he sighed as his vision blurred.

"Honey, you've lost a lot of blood—but don't worry, it'll come out in the wash," said Mom, understanding that for once it was the guy bleeding, not her.

"You've maimed me..." Dad muttered as he scrabbled for the brass knuckles on the nightstand.

"Hit her!" I screamed impotently from within my mother, who had begun to feel something as she watched my dad's cock bleed out and his face turn white. It was compassion, yes, but mingled with erotic desire. She fought the urge to touch herself. She had never seen damaged cock before.

"I'm bleeding out," said Dad, winding his fist back and getting ready to strike. "That sort of crap pisses me off. No wonder I'm preparing to act violently!"

"Hit her! She did this to you!" I yelled, but of course no one could hear me.

"I'm gonna hit you, no matter how unethical that seems—or how against the grain of the times," said Dad, his face reddening and his fist beginning to vibrate and engorge.

Cortisol flooded my system through the umbilical cord. Mom didn't want to be hit at all. The situation was stressing us out.

"I'm gonna do it. Soon..." Dad slurred.

"Do it now, you prevaricating bastard!" I yelled.

But his fist went flaccid and dropped. He'd lost too much blood.

Soon Dad followed his fist, collapsing into what a writer might call a "heap."

Mom, in her most shameful moment yet, which she believed was unwitnessed, brought herself to completion before calling 911. The father of her child was bleeding out and needed help.

"I guess I overdid it," I thought to myself ruefully. "But at least I helped Mom climax. I'm already 10 times the man Dad is, and I'm still but a shade."

But it wasn't over yet. Blinded and gagged by Dad's blood, I began to experience Mom's pleasure, not vicariously, but directly, as an extension of her, through the accursed umbilical—I began orgasming, much to my chagrin.

My wisp of a penis, undeveloped, achieved minor erection—but it was from within the mind (that most erogenous zone of the body, or so I'd heard) that I reached the height of pleasure. Soaring above my own consciousness, I experienced extreme vertigo. This was a kind of death, le petit mort, long-sought oblivion, euphoric and terrifying.

Was it possible that Mom was experiencing this very same feeling? The certainty that my mother and I were orgasming simultaneously made me convulse even harder. Together, I dissolved into we and nothing, that secret gaping absence within us, blossomed for the first time. I died, making love to my mother, and experienced nonexistence as something tangible, something sensual, something lived and experienced.

As I came down, the implications of my orgasm horrified me: nonbeing as fact precluded the experience of it. That which I sought, nonexistence, was attainable only on Earth as a carnal experience. I'd have to live to die.

Of course, some trace of a soul within me would always long for the Garden of Eden, that non-time when sperm and egg were forever separated. But I was beyond saving. Religion was for the spermatozoa, transcendent abstractions prior to or outside the world. In my pleasure principle, I found the richness of God here on earth, an immanent God coexistent with all things. A Father whose immanence was so absolute it was definitionally no different from absence. I knew that my life, the story of my *I*, was not going to be a *good* one. No one had ever pulled the project off well. Yet, life camouflaged itself in becoming colors, offering the likeness and prospect of death in the very act of its propagation. Hence its mass appeal.

Depleted from orgasm, me again, I lay back in the womb and experienced a growing contempt for my mother, the world around me, the one I loved. I wished I could stay here forever.

30 Rock

My boss knocked on the wall of my cubicle.

"How's that episode of 30 Rock or Brooklyn Nine-Nine coming along?" he asked.

"It's almost done," I said. "It just needs some punching up. The plot is pretty tightly structured at this point, but it isn't funny yet."

"I believe in you," said my boss, looking at me tenderly. "You're one of the funniest people I've ever had working under me. One day, perhaps, you'll be in my position. Just remember to have the episode on my desk by 5 pm. Oh, and you already know this, but remember that sometimes the truth is the funniest thing in the world. Write from your heart, Matthew."

I felt warmth course through my body after being praised. I scanned the script of the latest Brooklyn Nine-Nine or 30 Rock episode for places where I could insert jokes.

My friend Elias texted me and asked if I could talk.

"I'm at work," I texted back. "Can it wait?"

It couldn't.

Elias had recently gotten into a bad automobile accident and lost his legs. He called me periodically, wanting to talk urgently. The conversation would always ultimately be about mundane things. But I made time for him even while I was working because I knew he was depressed. I understood that for him, these conversations were acted out on a belated sense of urgency.

When I got off the phone, I had a dozen new ideas for the script. I wouldn't use Elias' name, but I'd use his pain. Comedy, I'd always opined, is simply tragedy plus time. Or from a distance. I decided that the newest draft of this 30 Rock episode would include several car crashes in the periphery of the screen, and they'd go hilariously unremarked upon by the supporting cast.

I got so involved in writing that I forgot to drink water! At a certain point, little pieces of dry skin started to fall from my chapped lips onto my paper. While dotting a T, my stylus ran into one of the flakes and got clogged. I shook my pen.

"This damn thing is clogged, and no ink is coming out," I said to no one before noticing that a couple of interns were reading over my shoulder and giggling.

"You are so funny," said the brunette. The brunette's graphic tee spoke volumes to me. It said *I Love New York*, something I have always fundamentally agreed with but never had the balls to say aloud. Below the text, a Statue of Liberty was dabbing.

"Love the shirt," I said, with a complicit smirk.

The other interns receded into the distance so I could be alone with the brunette who was still looking over my shoulder at my script.

"How d'you came up with that shit, because it's so damn funny?" she asked me.

"Writing and rewriting," I said. "And traveling while still young. Certain experiences stay with one for a lifetime."

"I'm twelve," she said. She described a recent experience with menses, one I was all too familiar with given the fact that by my thirties I'd had multiple long-term girlfriends.

"When I'm older, I want to go to Prague or Berlin, or perhaps—even better—somewhere with *no culture*," she said. "In my opinion, the least culturally rich places are those where culture has a capital C. Museums are sterile places; I prefer listening to the puerile musings of the working class."

"Well, yes," I said, taken aback. "I suppose anything can be fodder for a script. It's just a matter of being open to new experiences."

"I firmly believe," said my boss, suddenly stepping between us. "That people can have rich experiences even while staying at home."

"As long as they have iPhone privileges," his daughter laughed. My boss opened his palm. She pouted for a second and then placed her iPhone in his hand.

"You can wait in my office and do your homework," he said. "I'm dropping you off at your mom's house at 5:30."

"You should read Matthew's script," said the intern. Her dad grabbed it off my desk and flipped through it, stopping to grin at one of the longer passages.

"This line of reasoning is a bit out of character for Tina," he said. "It's outrageously funny, so maybe we'll leave it in. But otherwise, I think this script is good to go." He noticed that I was about to protest and cut me off. "Matthew. You're brilliant. This is incredible work. And don't forget that this is TV we're talking about, sort of lowest common denominator stuff. We're not writing the next great American novel. No one pays attention to what they're watching on TV. They're either stoned out of their minds or *Netflix and chilling*."

"Dad!" The intern looked appalled.

"Sorry, sorry." He turned to me. "Matthew, just go out, enjoy the day, spend time with your ex who you're still pretty good friends with. I'm officially giving you the rest of the day off. And anyway, it's true! You really did end things fairly amicably with your ex!"

I admitted it, and put my shit in my Jansport to get ready to bounce.

I sat in the office park briefly, chilling on my phone. It was 95 degrees, and my back sweated against the Jansport. A beautiful day though. Three birds in the air formed the points of a triangle; light rays shot out of the sun in all directions; two fluffy white clouds could be made out to the side. I looked out at the mountain that stretched from the horizon to the sky, with a two-story house on its highest peak. A man looked through the attic window and smiled. Behind the mountain: the ocean. Waves jostled each other gently. There were a few sailboats in the water but unfortunately a small shark fin circled the boats in a threatening manner.

Listlessly, I opened Instagram and flipped through my stories. I was putting off deciding what to do with my sudden influx of free time. The intern had teased me about whether I had any hobbies. I could go home and practice writing cop dialogue for Brooklyn Nine-Nine; would that count as a hobby? Ugh…

I swiped to the next Instagram story, which was about learning to love your cellulite. That didn't apply to me, but my ex had cellulite, so I screenshotted it and sent it to her. Things had ended on a good note between us.

The next Instagram story was about normalizing the use of baby formula, a goal I had always been down to work toward. I looked up from my phone and spaced out, thinking about my generation…

I was sitting on the edge of a round fountain that had three levels. The water sprayed up from the top, cascaded down to the second level, and finally rested on the bottom. The water was lit from below, and every few seconds, the hue of the light would change. A few stray dogs were drinking from the bowl at the bottom of the fountain.

"I'm so thirsty," someone said.

At first, I thought it was a dog. And then I realized it was just background audio. I turned around. Several of my co-writers were sitting on the grass among charcuterie fixings; one was smoking a spliff. They were pretty much all dressed in black.

"Here, sip this," one of them said. He pulled a flask out of his sock. "Come on, man. It's just water. Or rather, it looks like water."

"It's vodka, isn't it?" I said, smirking. They all grinned up at me.

"Matthew! Come join us! I know it's a bit of a sausage fest, but unfortunately, that's still how TV writers' rooms are. But we're having fun, we're drinking, and we're shooting the shit. Fuck it… Come through, man!"

I sat down with them for a second and even took a swig from Glen's flask.

"It's not entirely a sausage fest," said Martha. "Come on! I have a shit load of estrogen, though it is true that I produce a degree of testosterone too. Of course, my thyroid issues, among other things, sometimes affect the levels. Whatever, though. The relationship between sex hormones and gender is… complicated. But take my word for it—I'm all woman. Just look at these titties!"

She bounced up and down in a two-piece among all the men. Everyone laughed. The truth is, no one thought of anyone as a guy or a girl in the writer's room because what mattered was a person's sense of humor. In any case, it was hard to think about gender while laughing.

My coworkers sat on the grass, eating prosciutto, smoking cigarettes, and swigging vodka from Glen's flask. Outside the writer's room, away from Tina's watchful eye, they discussed cinema, literature, art world gossip, and politics. Glen rolled his eyes; Richard feigned outrage; Martha called her interlocutor a cynic. Their theatrics were well-rehearsed, their debates reheated.

I felt increasingly alone amidst the smiling crowd… What were they getting out of this, I wondered? I shared many of their interests and passions, but I didn't see the fun in making a game of them. I excused myself politely.

"I have to go home and feed my dog again," I said as they hugged me, and waved goodbye before fading into nothingness.

I returned to the fountain. I wasn't sure why. I looked wistfully up at a passing jet plane, which left a beautiful, white chemtrail in its wake. I reached into my pocket, picked out a penny, and tossed it up into the air. The penny flipped three, four, five times in mid-air then landed with a plop in the water.

"Don't forget to make a wish," I imagined someone saying.

"Oh, I didn't forget," I said out loud. "I most certainly made a wish!" I wished that something would finally happen to me. Because ugh—nothing ever happens to me.

—

When I got home and opened my door, I knew something wasn't right. The smell was overpowering.

It wasn't my dishes. I'd always been fastidious about doing them. In fact, with previous girlfriends, I'd always had a sort of unspoken arrangement. I would do the dishes, and in exchange, they would do the tasks that didn't come to mind because I wasn't raised to do them.

I walked into the laundry room. Nope! It wasn't the laundry... The smell was unmistakable. It was the unmistakable smell of death.

Ever since I was a kid, I've recognized that people never err when it comes to this stench, which is so horrible. The smell of death pisses one off so much that it makes people think of the worst thing imaginable: the death of a close friend or loved one. The idea of mistaking this smell for even a slightly more positive event, such as a maiming after a wreck, or a barely survivable knifing, is frankly unthinkable.

I knew someone had died in my home. I just had to figure out who...

In an attempt to brainstorm, I got out some of my old photo albums. I blew away the dust, making several guys in the distance cough. It had been years since I'd seen these. I looked at photos from my college graduation. Mom and Dad were in the photos, looking youthful. But had they died in my home? Doubtful. After all, I'd seen Dad at the nursing home recently... He seemed fine! And Mom... well, she had died when I was a kid. Though I wouldn't put it past her to do it again in my damn condo! She was literally that intrusive.

But no...

I scanned my uncle album. This was the album that had first motivated me to become a comedy writer. My funny uncles' eyes, ever smizing, gleamed and glimmered in the sepia photos. Surely, *these* men would never die.

So, who had?

I was about to give up when I stepped into my bedroom. Immediately, I knew that this room was the source of the putridity.

My dog lay there at the foot of my bed. His head was twisted dreadfully, tongue dangling out of his mouth and continuing to pulsate mournfully. His matted fur had grown long, as had his nails. He lay there in a pile of excrement and piss, his tail gone. Someone had sharpied the word "WHORE" on his ass. He had died of old age.

I sat down in my chaise lounge. I was stunned. I'd had my dog for 13 years, so it was pretty safe to say we'd formed a bond. But grief is strange. I must admit, my initial reaction was a feeling of betrayal. Why had my dog left me like that? I knew other feelings would soon emerge, but for now, I felt angry. I felt like saying bad dog. And at the thought of that, I began to cry.

I walked to the bathroom and looked in the mirror while I was peeing, admiring the depth of feelings my wet eyes represented. I hated that every time I cried, ever since I was a kid, I admired on some level my ability to reject toxic masculinity, even though I had never been rebuked for crying and had, in fact, gotten my way with it a lot.

My pee culminated in an impulse to dump. I turned around, sat down, performed the ritual, then took a hot steamy shower. Finishing my bedtime routine, I swallowed melatonin before moisturizing my face and getting into bed.

—

At work the next day, everything felt fuzzy. I barely remembered even driving there. I wrote several 30 Rock scripts on autopilot.

Returning from the cafeteria at the end of my lunch break, I was suddenly startled out of my reverie while feeding the caged actors some of my leftover fries. The lead, reaching through the cage's bars for anything to feed his artist's limitless appetite, eyed me ravenously.

"You look sad," he said.

"Huh. I guess I am sad."

It was just a moment. He and the other actors in their cage instantly began squabbling for the leftovers I'd thrown them, babbling in their theatrical way.

"It must just be their acting," I thought. "There's no way I look sad."

—

After finishing up my last script of the day, I knocked on my boss's office door. Hold on, he said from inside.

"It's Matthew."

"Oh, come in, come in.' I stepped inside and handed him my manuscripts.

"These are done. They need a little punching up from the zoomer interns, but structurally they're sound." I said, watching my boss flip through the pages.

"You're… done…?"

"Yes," I said. "Is it okay if I head out early again?"

"Sure, but…" My boss was concentrating on the pages. "These are excellent as always… Like all comedy plots, the plots transition from a state of disorder to one of order. Fitting for sitcoms, the characters don't change fundamentally by the end of each episode, which allows the show to continue indefinitely. But... Matthew. I've never known you to simply put scripts on my desk. Normally I have to tear them from you, you're such a perfectionist. What gives?"

"Eh," I said. "You're right. What you said yesterday. TV is just lowest common denominator stuff. I've mastered the craft of writing eps. So, unless you see anything objectionable about what I've handed you...?"

"No, no, it's all good, excellent stuff as always." My boss looked flustered.

"My boy," he said with a grave tone as he opened his drawer and took out a pinch of snuff, sniffing it twice. "Are you sure you're alright?"

"I'm good. Just... family trouble."

"So, I'm not the only one," he said. He looked relieved. "Listen, I'll let you off early, but can you drop off my daughter at her Go tutor's place? And then the rest of the day is yours. She's in the bathroom right now, but I can tell her to meet you in the lobby in 20–30 if you'd rather leave the office and wait by the fountains."

And there I was, sitting in the lobby by the fountain again. I examined the pennies inside of it, wondering which one was mine. An old man reading a newspaper looked up at me.

"The Taliban is at it again," he said.

"Oy," I said, as politely as possible.

"They're at it again," he said. "It's Western culture they take issue with."

"Eh, I'm just a TV writer," I said. "I don't know too much about that or anything, I just keep it funny…"

"A TV writer!" He scooted closer to me. "Listen, you're on the frontlines of this battle."

"How so?" I asked.

"Islam is the conclusion of thousands of years of monotheistic experimentation. Judaism and Christianity were too hesitant, too reluctant to think things through. If you believe in one God, there's no good reason to care about anything other than this supreme being. If you believe, it's only logical to devote every moment of your life to worship."

I listened intently; he had some good points!

"Coming from a protestant background, we Americans at first learned to subsume our worship into work. By working hard, we preempted predestination. Our pull-yourself-up-by-the-bootstraps ethic is just a mask for fatalism. If we succeed, it's because we were destined to. If we fail, it's because we're condemned. We work hard not to create, but to reveal our destinies."

"The great thing about TV," the old man said, lighting a cigarette. "It's an affront to God. When we watch TV and zone out—and let me stress that no TV has any redeeming value—we waste time. This precious time could be spent working or bettering ourselves. It's the opposite of the Protestant ethic's form of worship. Watching TV is anti-prayer!"

I waited for him to continue. He shrugged, returning to his newspaper. "As an atheist, I watch a lot of TV. Simpsons, Sopranos…"

"Who's this creep?" the child intern asked, sitting next to me.

"It's just an old man," I said. "He probably likes to diddle kids. So, stay well away."

"Gotcha," she said, covering her breasts, pussy, and asshole.

I could see the old man's face turn red behind his newspaper. The glow of his blush illuminated a particularly prescient op-ed. I felt a little bad.

A few minutes later my intern and I were zooming through the city in my Royce.

"Do you care if I wear a seatbelt?" I asked her, I hadn't been wearing one for the last 5 minutes.

"It's fine either way," said the child.

"How's your internship been going?" I asked her.

"Boring," she said. "Plus, I feel a little bad for the actors. It seems a little inhumane to keep them caged up like that in 2024."

"If it were up to me," I said, "every actor would be free to walk around the city as they please, lease apartments, and even get head. So, I'm 100% in agreement with you. But…"

"But! I'm so tired of hearing that word. You sound like my dad. His favorite word is, but."

"But… these reforms take time. As I'm sure you've heard before." With bitter irony, I pointed out an actor lying by the roadside, taking desultory swigs from a brown paper bag.

"This is what happens," I said, "when you just let them do as they please without a structure in place. The actors on our show are happy. On some level, they enjoy the discipline of work. It gives them something meaningful to do. Some of the smart ones even contribute lines of dialogue to the scripts sometimes!"

"Really? Like which lines?" She beamed.

"Well... remember the last episode where one of the side characters has a hacking cough? When he wiped the spittle off his shirt and sheepishly said, 'Sorry, sorry,' that was entirely improvised, even the hacking cough."

"That's awesome," she said. "I think I want to study acting one day."

"It's an interesting field," I said. "Are you more interested in the neurology of actors or their culture?"

"I think they're interrelated," she said. "But I'm more interested in applied acting. I want to harness actors for more socially useful ends, not just TV."

I could make out a pack of dogs drowning in a nearby lake through my Royce's tinted windows. I felt emotional.

"Nothing wrong with a bit of TV," I said defensively.

"Do you watch TV?" she asked me.

"Not much," I said. "Just write it."

"Well, what do you do?"

"Just hobbies and interests, like any normal person."

I parked the car and rolled up my suicide doors—which were manual. "We're here," I said. "Do you need me to walk you up?"

"No need to walk me there. I can *go* in myself," the intern said, unbuckling her seatbelt.

"That's very funny," I said. I shot her a look. "If you ever decide to become a TV sitcom writer, I'll have to watch my back."

"No need to worry about that," said the intern, turning back to me as she pranced up the garden pathway of her Go tutor's house. "I'm not interested, not in the least."

—

On the way home, I stopped by a dog shelter. Several dogs greeted me in the parking lot as soon as I opened my suicide doors. They licked me and wagged their tails.

"They like you," said a staff member, slowly walking up. "What do you have that I lack?"

Two of the dogs turned back to glare at him. The staff member flashed me a grin.

"They think I'm pedantic. Name's Tom." I shook his hand. "You here to adopt a dog?"

"Yeah. Mine actually passed away. Old Age is a bitch. Or was a bitch, before I found her corpse the other day. It was my dog's namesake that killed her in the end, I must confess. So, I'm looking for a new one."

"These dogs," said Tom, "are looking for what we like to call a *forever home*. A sort of place that they can never leave. May I ask what you do for a living?"

"I'm a TV writer," I said.

"No shit," said Tom, sitting down behind his big desk and indicating a sofa for me. "What show?"

"Some sitcom, 30 Rock or Brooklyn Nine-Nine."

"I love those shows," he said. "I watch them with my family on a nightly basis. You see, I'm the sort of guy with a wife and kids."

"Shocker," I said, gesturing toward his ring and his postpartum scars.

"We love the dialogue you cook up for Tina and her friends to utter," said Tom. "It's charmingly off-kilter. My kids especially like the side characters who are on the younger side. But my wife and I are fans of the show's consistency, the way the relationships between the main characters develop without ever, y'know, developing."

"It's a job," I said. "I just happen to be very good at it."

Tom leaned back in his chair.

"I feel like I'm meeting a celebrity," he said. "I can't wait to tell my wife and kids that I gave a dog or dogs to one of the Brooklyn Nine-Nine or 30 Rock writers. Listen. I won't ask you for an autograph. That would be too gauche. But would you ever... No, nevermind, stupid to even ask."

"What?"

"Would you be willing to meet my wife and kids?"

"Are they good company?"

"They help pass the time when I'm not here working at the dog shelter. It would be a super quick meet and greet. We can meet in the city square on Sunday. What do you say?"

"On Sunday, I planned on rewriting some old 30 Rock episodes for posterity's sake. I don't have time for family stuff, anyway. Can you just show me to the dogs?"

"I understand," said Tom, suddenly coughing a decent amount. He'd been a heavy smoker in his youth.

He opened his office door, and several of the most loving dogs I'd ever seen stepped in. They licked me up and down, and I had them roll over. We did drills. I examined their bodies for defects. Ultimately, I decided to let them languish in the shelter forevermore, aside from one I named and took home with me as an official possession.

My replacement dog smelled the same as my previous one. He could consistently smell or hear guys approaching the house with what he believed to be ill intent. Whether his senses were accurate or not was beside the point. I liked having an animal in my home who saw signs of malice everywhere and loved only me.

—

After several weeks with my dog, I realized I didn't love him back. I loved my previous dog but not my new one, even though they both relished the same slop and acted alert around threats.

At work, one day, I inserted myself into my 30 Rock scripts. I wrote episodes where Tina Fey drove to and from work, ate quiet meals between work shifts, and replaced dog after dog ad infinitum to great comedic effect.

"Something feels like it's missing," said Tina to a black guy. She smiled sadly at a gay guy, who looked at the camera and winked. She spent the remainder of the season isolating.

—

I thought more and more about Tom's family. I imagined them alert at the dinner table, sensibly keeping their ears pricked for neighborhood threats.

"Your work isn't exactly declining." My boss was talking to me. "There's just a quiet sadness to it now. Audiences eat this up, naturally. It's very de rigueur. But I'm worried about you."

"I'm fine," I said. "I just feel very much alone, boss."

"I want you to take a week off," he said. "Take some time to think about how you want to live. Think about what would make it more meaningful to you… if anything. It's okay if the answer is nothing; we need you here; Tina needs you; the actors need you; the world audience needs you."

—

When I got home that night, I fed my dog and then myself. I took a Xanax and stared out the window at the world audience. At midnight, I called the dog shelter.

"Is Tom there?"

"Tom speaking."

"Hey, it's Matthew Goldin, the TV writer who came in the other day—do you remember me? I think… I think I'm ready to meet your family."

"Of course, I remember you! And yes! Why don't you have dinner with us tomorrow night? My wife is boiling something we'll *all* enjoy. The kids will have learned something new in school that day.

I, meanwhile, ever the traditionalist, will provide for the financial aspect of the evening, as well as do ill by my wife once you are gone."

"And I'll be the treasured guest?"

"Very much treasured."

I grinned silently and hung up the phone. "I'll see you then," I said forcefully.

—

When I arrived, I saluted the house's Amazon Ring camera with a flourish.

Home security systems reminded me of sex toys. Both were the works of technology on some fundamental level, and both of them did a man's job.

I felt sick as the Ring camera's lens extended to focus on me. I ignored it, feeling suddenly bereft and impotent in the certainty that the Ring would not deem me a threat.

"I'm armed," I said jokingly to a neighbor hosing off his little garden. A part of the world audience, the man's curious smile turned into a grin as he digested the humor of what I'd said.

The ring light turned green, and the door rotated in some convoluted sci-fi manner to let me in. Greeting me at the door, Tom's wife, wheelchair-bound, offered me her cheek, which I bent down and kissed dryly.

"You must be Matthew," she said, in a welcoming yet vaguely peremptory way, as if I might decide to be someone else for the remainder of the evening.

She introduced me to her children, two iPhone-bound boys whose faces the censors had blurred.

"They're interchangeable," said Tom's wife.

"We all are," said Tom, appearing in the room to hand me a beer. "But that doesn't mean we shouldn't introduce ourselves."

"I'm Eustace," she said, turning pale. She always forgot shit like that. Ever since she was a kid.

"Understood," I replied.

I watched Tom watch me take a sip of the beer he'd handed me.

Satisfied, he suggested we all have a seat on the back patio while his wife finished seasoning the dinner.

"I want to add the salt!"—"No, me!" I heard the kids screaming and fighting.

Tom and I took our seats in front of the backyard's abyss. He turned to me and discussed pussy for a moment, followed by current events. "How's your dog treating you?" he asked, without relish.

"Truly a master's pet," I said blandly.

"Quite so, quite so." He was drifting off.

"And your family?" I asked. "Tell me, honestly, what is it like having a family?"

"And living in the 'burbs?" he said, laughing—and then coughing, to a concerning degree. 'Best decision I ever made."

I looked down into the abyss, the walls of which gloomy and self-serious scribes had covered with their tedious graffiti.

Eustace wheeled herself out. She blinked to indicate that dinner was ready. Her paralysis had begun to spread.

Tom and I followed Eustace in.

We sat down at our places at the table. Eustace, of course, was already sitting.

"I have a fairly solid read on the cultural thermometer," I said, "so there won't be any gratuitous wheelchair jokes from me today."

"My husband is similar," Eustace said, smiling. "He understands where the culture's at, so he rarely makes fun of my condition."

"We all have our own conditions. Why punch down?"

"What condition do you have, Dad?" said Tom's son.

"Benign prostatic hyperplasia." Tom grinned. "You'll understand when you're older."

"Sounds like philosophy major mumbo jumbo," his son said, raising an eyebrow. "I don't fetishize illness."

"You did when you were a baby," his mother said. "You had croup."

"What is croup?"

"Basically," said Eustace, "You had a distinctive barking cough. As we pushed you down the street in your stroller, you made a harsh sound, known technically as a 'stridor,' each time you breathed in. You also found it very difficult to breathe in general."

"Almost didn't make it, huh," said the child, age 12.

"Almost not," said Tom, serving himself another helping of boiled groceries.

We sat there silently for a moment before quickly addressing a series of disparate topics.

The family was eating very messily. They were getting food all over the place. There were no family dogs to gobble it up from below, so something else (unclear) took care of the droppings instead.

"What do you think of us?" ssked Eustace. "In all honesty."

I stood up.

"Tolstoy once wrote, 'All happy families resemble one another, but each unhappy family is unhappy in its own way.'"

"Cut the crap," said Eustace. "We've all read Anna Karenina. I want to know what you think; don't rest on the laurels of your reading."

"Okay," I said. "I'll be honest. I'm jealous. I never wanted a family. All I ever wanted was to be a bachelor and to have my career go quite swimmingly. But when I'm not working, I feel like something is missing—and my dog doesn't cut it. I never feel lonely, though."

Eustace nodded. "That's what's missing: loneliness. It is difficult to be alone after childhood," she said. "Childhood is lonely because you are framed by a family that is increasingly ill-fitting. You're forced to go to school to do any number of things. You are the only real thing in a strange, impersonal world that constantly imposes itself on you."

"But when you become an adult," she continued, "when you become autonomous, the world is yours, at least in theory. The people in your life are people you've chosen. Your activities are, at least in theory, your true passions. If you achieve some semblance of success and can afford to have your own space, you fill it entirely. Drowning in yourself, you never have any solitude or space for yourself. You start missing loneliness."

"Family," said Tom, "is a frame. Something to always surround you. An affirmed not-you, a chosen strangeness."

He smiled at his wife and his family. "I only remember to love them insofar as they remain strangers to me," he said.

"Well put, both of you," I said, clapping with slow-style sarcasm.

"My parents like you," said one of the sons. "Like, *like-like* you. They probably want a threesome or crap like that. At the very least, they're trying to impress you with this little performance." The tween spat on his parents. "Edgelord dweebs," he said, before excusing himself to go jack off quietly in his room again.

"I couldn't agree more," I said, standing up. "What you've said is ridiculous. Family is family. It's as simple as that."

Tom put his hands in the air like I was trying to shoot him. "I think what we were saying wasn't necessarily anti-family. We were just coming at it from an interesting angle. We knew it was somewhat provocative, though."

"Family is family," I reiterated, standing up. "And you should be grateful for what you have. I've never taken a stand on anything before, but I will right here. Treasure your wife and your children, Tom. They will be with you forever up until the moment you die. And if they die first, they will await you in Heaven—if you're a religious type."

Everyone shook my hand and wished me luck. Our time together had been a raging success.

When I got home, I found my replacement dog dead. He was hanging from the banister. He felt something had been off for many years, and he'd never been able to put his finger on it. His ghost circled his corpse, looking for bones.

"Unfinished business," it said, mirthlessly.

—

I decided not to get another dog.

I did get a call from my friend Elias while I was at work, though. I quickly regretted answering. His recovery, he explained, was going swimmingly. His legs had begun to grow back. I listened to him drone on and on about them. "They help me move," he said at length. "Or they will, once they finish developing, a process I never get tired of observing. I can't wait to cycle between my apartment and work with these legs."

Not once did he ask me a single question about my life. I made an excuse and got off the phone. Someday soon an accident would again render him a friend.

I returned to my Brooklyn Nine-Nine or 30 Rock script.

Tina Fey, I wrote, was having a bad day. Lying in bed, she stared at her laptop and listlessly opened up another tab. To pass the time, she clicked to a website that promised to depict actors with great liberty. Tina spent the remainder of the episode on this website.

A few hours later, my boss called me over into his office. A blonde in sunglasses and a pantsuit sat across from him.

"This is Sheila," my boss said. He cleared his throat. "She's very interested in the website you mention in your script."

"Sheila, FBI," she said by way of introduction.

"The website? Oh! It was a joke," I said. "And a bad one. Obviously, Tina would never jerk it to actors."

"Oh shit," she said. "I totally misunderstood."

My boss smiled. "What did I tell you?" he said to the FBI agent. "He's a good kid."

My boss took a pinch of snuff, sneezed.

"I feel like an idiot," said Sheila. "I'm really angry with myself for how literally I took your script. I know I've seriously wasted your time. I'm a low-quality FBI agent. I'm sorry."

"There's no need to apologize," I said. I looked at my boss. Despite obviously working to hold back another sneeze, he managed to wink at me. "Look, uh… Sheila, was it? You can make it up to me by going out with me this Friday. Do you like romantic dinners?"

Sheila turned beet red fetchingly.

"I do," she said. "It's been my favorite food ever since I was a kid."

"I'll pick you up at 8," I prophesied.

At 8, I drove by the agent's apartment. She lived in the ghetto. I texted her that I was there. A minute later, the door opened. She stood at the threshold, feeling herself for a moment, admiring her own agency.

The agent entered my car, looking sexy to me personally.

"Let's drive," she said.

My Royce went into action, getting to the destination in record time.

"Let's do this thing," I said to the waiter once we were seated, exuding charm so he'd get us the best food.

"What are you hungry for?" he asked us. "Like, what sort of food."

"Italian," the agent and I said simultaneously.

"Jinx," I said, depriving her of her voice forevermore—and making her my wife.

Our eyes met. And time, petrified by fear, froze—before dashing into overdrive.

—

"Brilliant work," said my boss, startling me. He was looking over my shoulder. As usual, I was hunched over the latest 30 Rock or Brooklyn Nine-Nine Script. "Sorry, didn't mean to break your concentration," he said.

I dotted an m and turned around. "Sorry to keep you waiting," I said, "I just wanted to make sure this episode was perfect."

"No harm done," said my boss. "I'm just happy that you're once again writing in your inimitable style."

"You think the situations I put Tina and the other actors into are funny?"

"Yeah! Of course! The situations are insane!"

My boss tried to take the script off my desk but I slapped his hand away. "Sorry," I said. "I just want to make things a bit more arduous for Tina, if you don't mind? I really want to see her squirm in this ep... Things will go awry before returning, naturally, to a state of equilibrium. I just want to stay in the office for a few more hours to work on this."

"I have a better idea," said my intern, stepping into the cubicle. "Allow me," she said, shadowboxing theatrically, "to punch up your script."

My boss raised an eyebrow. "That's a lot of responsibility, you know..."

"Um yeah, I know, Dad," said the intern. "Except I've been working here like 6 months and I think I have the tone and rhythm of the show down pat by now. It's just TV, jeez. Pretty lowest common denominator stuff. Plus I'll bring a fresh youthful perspective to the show."

"What do you think, Matthew?" asked my boss with a deferential little sniff.

"I mean, she's not wrong," I said.

"Thank you, Matthew!" she squealed.

"I thought you didn't want to be a TV writer," I said.

"I don't, but it looks good on college applications. Please, just let me do it! I already have, like, a billion ideas for Tina. For instance, I want to make her breathe really slowly for an entire episode—quite inexplicably."

"That's very funny actually," I said. "Well, it's ultimately up to your dad." I turned to my boss. "I honestly can't see the harm in having her punch up the script. If you're okay with it."

"Matthew," he said. "Of course I'm okay with it. I just want you out of this office. You're making the rest of us look lazy. Get some rest. Or go to the municipal pool with that new wife of yours. Sheila, right? You two have been hitting it off lately, no? Or, I forget—are you in a rough patch?"

"We are in a rough patch. yeah."

It was true. While I was glad to have nabbed a wife, I missed the strong independent FBI agent I'd met the week before. Upon getting married, she'd immediately quit the agency to focus on being subjugated by me full-time. In fact, she made grim work of the pun by taking a firm stance against the very concept of agency in a series of Medium essays, which were well circulated in trad circles.

"All the more reason why you should spend the rest of the day at the community pool or the beach—or some body of water. *Go.*"

My intern was grinning silently, obviously stunned by her opportunity. It brought me back to my early days of writing for SNL.

"Go," said my boss, shooing me off. "We'll be fine here!"

I put my shit in my Jansport and got ready to bounce. On the way out, I stopped by the lobby fountain to collect myself and text my wife an invitation to the beach.

The old man was sitting by the fountain again.

He crumpled his newspaper up into a big ball and threw it up in the air. It hung suspended in the air for a few minutes, spinning slowly, while he formulated his wish. Then it fell with a thud into the water, absorbing water and expanding so that it formed a gelatinous paste that all but filled the fountain. Some of the actors playing inside of the fountain screamed.

"I can't move," moaned a tubby actor in his mid-thirties.

Nor, I thought to myself, *could I*, relating for the first time in my life to a thespian.

Without enthusiasm, I drove to the beach. My wife was already there when I arrived. She wore big sunglasses. I kissed her clumsily on the lips.

"This is nice," I said, sitting down next to her and feeling the sand between my toes.

"It is," she said, before mentioning kids.

In the car, on the way back from the beach, I gave my wife the silent treatment. I wasn't mad. The "silent treatment" was my term for when I went inside my head to play with dogs. I threw balls for them, patted them until they rolled onto their backs, and then patted their bellies, and even groomed them, sometimes for hours at a time. I'd always done this. Imagining dogs and the many ways of interacting with them had always been a great way to punish my loved ones.

When we got home, I made my amends. We talked things out. Afterward, sexuality and humor combined and charmed us into having intercourse with each other.

We did dirty talk and pretended, for a moment, to be actors. Condoms, she said, represented the slow cancellation of the future. I experienced horror but was turned on by her pretension. She used her vibrator to stimulate her clit while she rode me. The credits began rolling. I hadn't even cum yet. The names of the people responsible for all this flashed across the screen.

I knew, of course, that if I didn't shut everything down right then and there, the next episode would automatically begin. Things would be different and yet the same.

Out of passivity and boredom, I stayed where I was. This was lowest common denominator stuff, sure, but there was nothing else to do.